CODING BASICS

Coding Basics: Understanding Medical Collections

CODING BASICS

Coding Basics: Understanding Medical Collections

Michelle M. Rimmer, CHI
President
Professional Medical Billers Association
Brick, New Jersey

Australia • Brazil • Japan • Korea • Mexico • Singapore • Spain • United Kingdom • United States

Coding Basics: Understanding Medical Collections
Michelle M. Rimmer

Vice President, Career and Professional Editorial: Dave Garza

Director of Learning Solutions: Matthew Kane

Senior Acquisitions Editor: Rhonda Dearborn

Managing Editor: Marah Bellegarde

Product Manager: Jadin Babin-Kavanaugh

Editorial Assistant: Chiara Astriab

Vice President, Career and Professional Marketing: Jennifer McAvey

Executive Marketing Director: Wendy Mapstone

Senior Marketing Manager: Nancy Bradshaw

Marketing Coordinator: Erica Ropitzky

Production Director: Carolyn Miller

Production Manager: Andrew Crouth

Content Project Manager: Brooke Baker

Senior Art Director: Jack Pendleton

Technology Product Manager: Mary Colleen Liburdi

Library of Congress Control Number: 2008944319

ISBN-13: 978-1-4283-7794-3

ISBN-10: 1-4283-7794-8

Delmar
5 Maxwell Drive
Clifton Park, NY 12065-2919
USA

Cengage Learning is a leading provider of customized learning solutions with office locations around the globe, including Singapore, the United Kingdom, Australia, Mexico, Brazil, and Japan. Locate your local office at **international.cengage.com/region**

Cengage Learning products are represented in Canada by Nelson Education, Ltd.

To learn more about Delmar, visit **www.cengage.com/delmar**

Purchase any of our products at your local college store or at our preferred online store **www.ichapters.com**

Printed in United States of America
1 2 3 4 5 6 7 12 11 10 09

Contents

Reviewers ix

Preface xi

Dedication xv

Acknowledgements xvii

Chapter 1 When Does Collecting Begin? 3

How the Collection Process Works 4

Patient Registration 4

Protecting the Practice with a Financial Policy 5

The Next Step in the Collections Process 9

The Role of the Collections Clerk 9

The Role of Customer Service in Collections 9

Effective Communications 11

Implementing a Plan 11

Chapter 2 Legal Guidelines for Collecting 15

Medical Debt 16

Federal and State Regulations 16

Frequently Asked Questions for Collection Practices 16

Prohibited Practices 17

Chapter 3 Aging Reports and the Department of Insurance 23

The Aging Process 24

Insurance Aging Reports 27

Follow-up 29
Using the Internet 29
Telephone Calls 30
Re-billing 31
Regulating Insurance Companies 31
Complaints 31
Patient Aging Report 34
Consistency 36

Chapter 4 In-Office Patient Collection Strategies 45

Health Insurance Verification 46
Co-insurance 46
Medicare 46
Co-payment 46
The Uninsured Patient 48
Forms of Payment 49
Post-dated Checks 49
Payment Arrangements 49
Patient Statements 49
Calling the Patient 52

Chapter 5 The Appeal Process 61

The Denied Claim 62
The Appeal Process: Responding to the Denied Claim 62
Appeals Documentation 65

Chapter 6 Additional Income for the Medical Office 73

Supplemental Sources of Income 74
Medical Records Copying 74
Form Completion 74
Narrative Report 75
Missed Appointment Fee 75
Medical Expert Witness 84
Range of Fees 85

Chapter 7 Selecting an Outside Collection Agency 89

The Role of a Collection Agency 90

Selecting a Collection Agency 90

Collection Techniques 90

Collection Agency Fees 94

The Importance of Communication 94

Maintaining Customer Service 94

Appendix I Student Exercises 97

Appendix II Forms, Lists, and Tables 101

Appendix III CMS-1500 Claim Filing Instructions 131

Appendix IV Patient's Bill of Rights 143

Appendix V Medical Terminology Review 145

Roots, Prefixes, and Suffixes 145

Roots 145

Prefixes 148

Suffixes 149

Glossary 151

Index 155

Reviewers

The author and publisher would like to thank the following reviewers for their feedback:

Deborah Fazio, CMAS, RMA
Medical Billing and Coding Program Director
Sanford Brown Institute
Middleburg Heights, Ohio

Rashmi Gaonkar, MS (Chemistry)
Senior Instructor/ASA Institute
Brooklyn, New York

Jacqueline A. Howard, CPC, CPC-H, CCS-P, CMBA
The Coding Source
Santee, California

Sharon Imperiale CMA, AA Science
Instructor
College America
Phoenix, Arizona

Norma Mercado, MAHS, RHIA
Department Chair, Austin Community College
Austin, Texas

Pat G. Moeck, PhD, MBA, BA, CMA (AAMA)
Director, Medical Assisting Program
El Centro College
Dallas, Texas

Julie Pope, CMA (AAMA), CPC, CPC-H, CPC-I
Program Director/ATA Career Education
Louisville, Kentucky

Preface

Effective collections in the medical office are a vital function in maintaining accounts receivable and a steady cash flow. *Coding Basics: Understanding Medical Collections* provides the knowledge necessary for the collections process in the medical office, from the beginning—when the patient calls to schedule an appointment—to the end, with payment of the claim or sending the claim to an outside collection agency.

This textbook includes hands-on exercises, aging reports, denial and appeal letters, and common debt collection terms to familiarize you with the collections process. It also covers Federal collection laws, HIPAA, and the appeals process.

FEATURES OF THE TEXTBOOK

Coding Basics: Understanding Medical Collections is part of the Coding Basics series of books from Delmar, Cengage Learning, designed to provide the basic training needed for employment in a physician's office. These basics can be taught at the vocational, college, and career-school levels, in either a traditional or modular program.

This worktext includes the following features:

- Role-playing scenarios for face-to-face and telephone dialogue for real-life collection techniques for both insurance and patient collections
- "Stop and Analyze" questions to encourage active student participation in learning the subject material
- Hands-on exercises for practice with aging reports and the claims appeals process
- Examples of both verbal and non-verbal means of communications to maintain a high level of customer service for patients of the medical practice
- A list of frequently asked questions and answers regarding the legal guidelines for collections
- Tables provided for specific state guidelines regarding collecting monies due the medical practice

Organization of the Textbook

- Chapter One, When does Collecting Begin?, explains the importance of collecting and verifying the patients' health insurance information prior to being seen in the office and why doing so can reduce the need for future collections.
- Chapter Two, Legal Guidelines for Collecting, answers some frequently asked questions regarding collection protocol and provides guidelines found in the Fair Debt Collections Practices Act.
- Chapter Three, Aging Reports and the Department of Insurance, provides sample insurance and patient aging reports for student practice. This chapter introduces the Department of Insurance and how the medical office can seek help with each state's department to assist in getting outstanding health insurance claims paid.
- Chapter Four, In-office Patient Collection Strategies, introduces methods for collecting payments. Role-playing scenarios are provided for face-to-face and telephone collections encounters with patients.
- Chapter Five, The Appeal Process, explains the necessary steps in appealing a denied claim. Sample appeal letters are provided, as well as an exercise for students to write their own appeal letter to an insurance payer.
- Chapter Six, Additional Income for the Medical Office, provides examples of how the office can collect additional money to increase cash flow for the office; these include charging for form completion (sports physicals, pre-employment physicals, narrative reports).
- Chapter Seven, Selecting an Outside Agency, includes factors to consider when deciding to hire a collection agency to assist in collecting money due from patients.

Referenced websites

- www.donself.com
- www.lamblawoffice.com
- www.cms.gov
- www.ftc.gov
- www.healthproconsulting.net
- www.pwwemslaw.com

ABOUT THE AUTHOR

Michelle M. Rimmer is a Certified Healthcare Instructor with over 19 years of experience in the medical billing field. She has taught numerous courses and seminars at three colleges in the state of New Jersey. In March of 2008, Michelle started the *Professional Medical Billers Association*, a networking group for medical billing students, professional medical billers, and medical billing business owners; the association offers both online courses and onsite courses in Lakewood, New Jersey. Michelle operated her own home-based medical billing company, *Shore Medical Billing,* for 11 years and recently started her new company, *Shore Medical Consulting Services.* Her passion for teaching medical billing led to the fruition of Michelle's first textbook, *Medical Billing 101.*

Dedication

This book is dedicated to my students, both online and in the classroom. Thank you for your enthusiasm *for* and dedication *to* learning!

Acknowledgments

I would like to thank the following people:

- Irene Malfitano—my "speed demon typist".
- The staff at Cengage Learning—Rhonda Dearborn, for taking a second chance on me; Jadin Babin-Kavanaugh, for her never ending assistance, and Chiara Astriab, for her quick responses to all my questions!
- MaryAnne Dauphin—thank you for "riding" my dream with me; you are a true class act, a great instructor, and a wonderful friend.
- My husband, Mike, and our three daughters: Chelsea, Alyssa, and Megan—thanks for understanding how important *Mom's* projects are and for sharing my excitement!

AVENUE FOR FEEDBACK

The author may be contacted by email at LMBOADM@aol.com

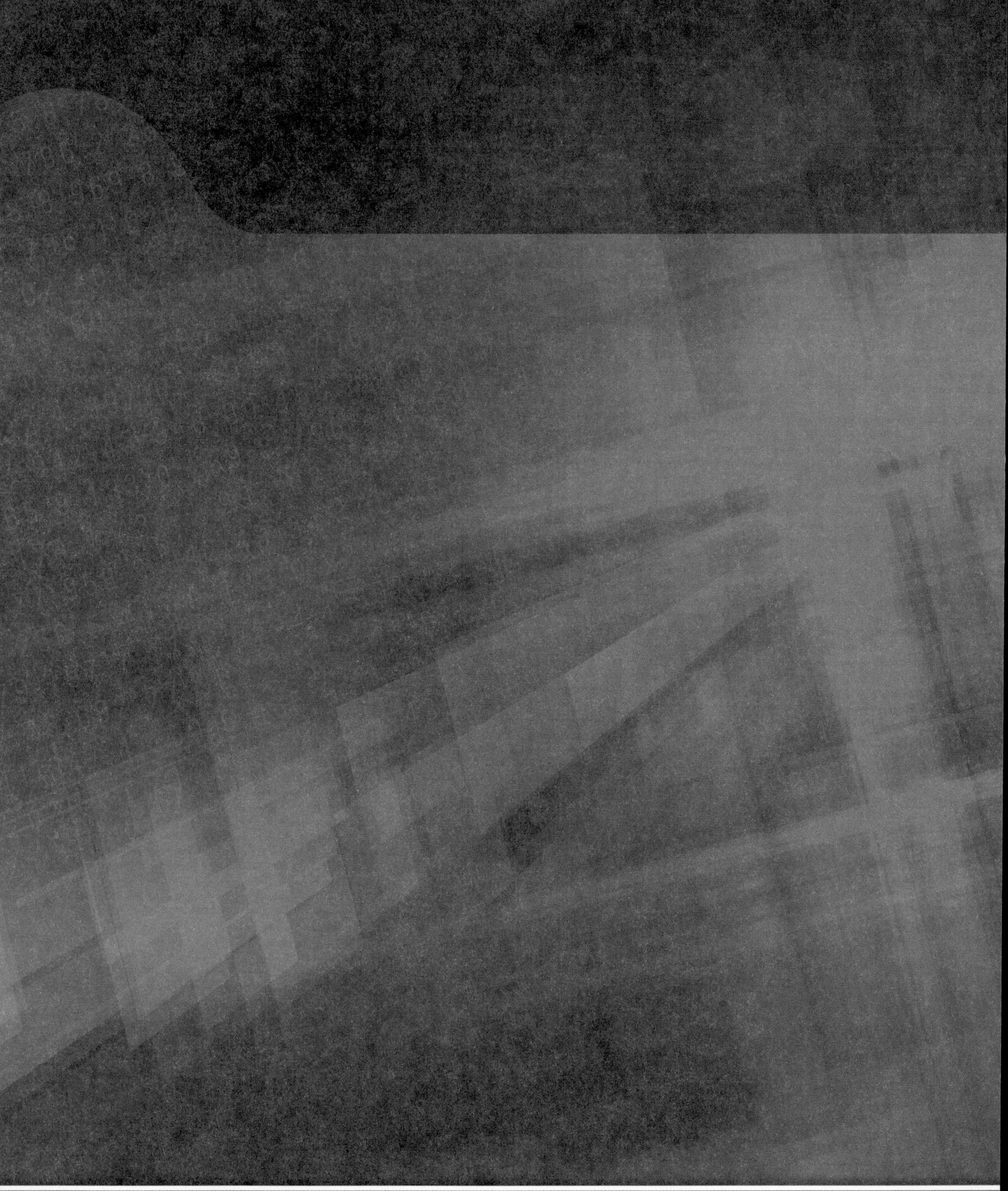

Chapter 1

When Does Collecting Begin?

OBJECTIVES

Upon completion of this chapter, the student should be able to:

- Explain the steps in the collections process.
- Discuss the importance of establishing a financial policy.
- Describe the job duties of a collections clerk.
- Understand the role customer service plays in the collection process.

KEY TERMS

Accounts receivable
Age
Appeal letters
Appeal process
Assignment of benefits
Collecting
Collections clerk
Co-insurance
Co-payment
Customer service
Deductible
Financial policy
Guarantor
Health insurance
Health insurance claim
Identification number

KEY TERMS

New patient

Outsourced

Patient registration form

Self-pays

State insurance commissioner

Subscriber

HOW THE COLLECTION PROCESS WORKS

The process of collecting, claiming what is due and receiving payment, can actually begin before the patient is ever seen in the medical office. This is true for offices that verify patients' health insurance prior to the first visit. Health insurance is defined as a contract between the subscriber (the person who "carries" the health insurance) and the insurance company to pay for medical care and preventive services.

During the telephone call to schedule an appointment, medical staff should obtain the health insurance identification number (the number listed on the health insurance card) that identifies the patient to the insurance company. The identification card may include:

- Subscriber's name
- Patient's name
- Identification number
- Group or plan number (if the insurance is through an Employer Group Health Plan)
- Effective date of coverage
- Co-payment (a flat fee the patient pays each time for medical services; associated with managed care plans)
- Co-insurance (a percentage amount the patient is responsible to pay for cost of medical services; associated with fee-for-service or traditional plans)
- Deductible amount (the dollar amount the patient is responsible to pay before any reimbursement is made by the insurance company)
- Name, address, and telephone number of the insurance company

See Figure 1-1.

Possession of health insurance information prior to the scheduled appointment better enables the office in the collection process, as it will then be known and can subsequently be noted on the patient's medical chart if there is a deductible to be met, a co-payment amount due, if the patient is responsible to pay a percentage of the visit or procedure.

Patients without health insurance and who must pay out-of-pocket for medical care are called self-pays. Because self-pay patients are expected to pay for medical care at the time services are rendered, the collections process for these patients should begin and end on the day of the office visit.

Patient Registration

On the day of the appointment, the new patient (one who has never been seen before, or who has not been seen in the past 36 months) will be required

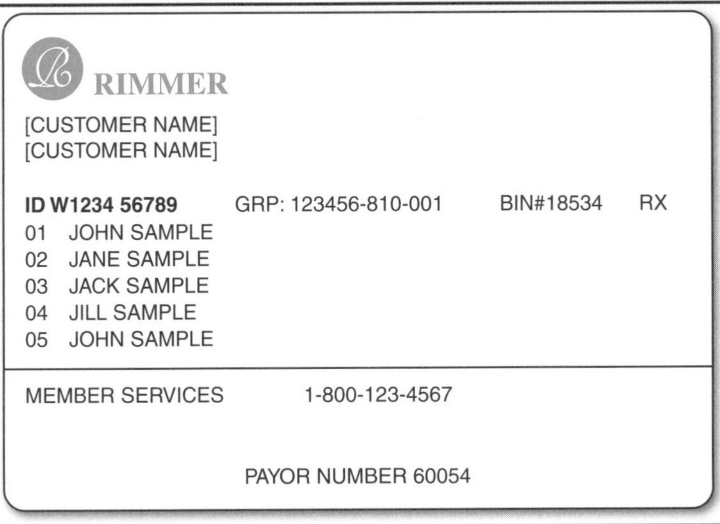
RIMMER
[CUSTOMER NAME]
[CUSTOMER NAME]

ID W1234 56789	GRP: 123456-810-001	BIN#18534	RX
01 JOHN SAMPLE			
02 JANE SAMPLE			
03 JACK SAMPLE			
04 JILL SAMPLE			
05 JOHN SAMPLE			

MEMBER SERVICES 1-800-123-4567

PAYOR NUMBER 60054

Figure 1-1. Sample health insurance identification card

to fill out a **patient registration form** (a form used to gather all patient information, including demographics and insurance information). This form should require:

- Patient's full legal name
- Demographics
- Employment information
- Emergency contact
- Health insurance information
- **Guarantor** (person financially responsible for the patient's account)

See Figure 1-2.

A fully completed patient registration form is an important tool to aid in the collections process. If contact information is left off this form, it can increase the difficulty in collecting money from a patient if the need arises.

During the registration process, medical office personnel should also make a photocopy of the front and back of the health insurance identification card to be placed in the patient's medical chart.

PROTECTING THE PRACTICE WITH A FINANCIAL POLICY

One of the greatest tools used to assist in the collections process is the medical practice's **financial policy**. The financial policy is a formal set of rules and

Practice Name

PATIENT REGISTRATION

Welcome to our office. In order to serve you properly, we will need the following information. **(Please Print)**
All information will be strictly confidential.

Patient's Name	Sex M F	Birth Date ___/___/_____ Age_________	Marital Status Single [ ] Married [ ] Widowed [ ] Divorced [ ]
Residence address City State Zip		Home Phone:	Patient's Social Security #
Person financially responsible for this account	Self Spouse Parent	Responsible Party's Birthdate ___/___/_____	Responsible Party's Social Security #
Responsible Party Drivers License # State: Number		Occupation	How Long at current Employer?
Credit Card: Number: Type [ ] Mastercard [ ] Visa [ ] Discover		Expiration Date:	Name On Card
Name of employer Address		Business Phone	Occupation
Name of Spouse/Parent	Birth date	Social security #	Business phone
Reason for Visit:	Referred by: (include address and phone)		
Person to contact in case of emergency:	Relationship to patient	Phone	
Medicare Yes [ ] No [ ]	Medicare #	Medicaid Yes [ ] No [ ]	Medicaid #	Effective Date
Medicare Secondary insurance name Address		Policy #	Group #
Workers' Compensation? Yes [ ] No [ ] Motor Vehicle? Yes [ ] No [ ] **If Yes-put W/C or MVA carrier below**	Date of Accident	Treatment authorized by	Claim #	W/C or MVA Insurance Phone #
Primary insurance company Address		Is insurance through your employer?	
Subscriber Name	Subscriber birth date	Policy #	Group #
Secondary insurance name Address		Policy #	Group #

Medicare Lifetime Signature on File:
I request that payment of authorized Medicare benefits be made on my behalf to Practice Name for any services furnished me by the physician. I authorize any holder of medical information about me to release to the Health Care Financing Administration and its agents any information to determine these benefits payable for related services

Patient Signature ______________________ Date ______________

Private Insurance Authorization for Assignment of Benefits/Information Release:
I, the undersigned authorize payment of medical benefits to Practice Name for any services furnished me by the physician. I understand that I am financially responsible for any amount not covered by my contract. I also authorize you to release to my insurance company or their agent information concerning health care, advice, treatment or supplies provided to me. This information will be used for the purpose of evaluating and administering claims of benefits.

Patient, Parent or Guardian Signature (if child is under 18 years old) ______________________ Date ______________

Figure 1-2. Sample patient registration form

procedures that the practice follows with regards to collecting money. The following should be included in the financial policy statement:

- Consent for treatment and authorization to release information
- Insurance coverage waiver—this means that although the office will submit claims to the health insurance company, the patient is ultimately responsible for the bill
- Assignment of benefits (authorization for payment to be made directly to the provider)
- Co-pay policy
- Cancellation/no show policy
- Self-pay policy
- Late fee or interest charges for overdue patient bills
- Acceptable forms of payment

See Figure 1-3.

The financial policy statement should be given at the time of registration, signed by the patient or guarantor, and placed in the patient's medical chart.

A thorough understanding of the practice's financial policy is not only important for the patients of the practice but for the entire medical staff as well so they are clear about their roles in the collections process.

Practice Name
Statement of Patient Financial Responsibility

Patient Name: ______________________________ **DOB:** ____________

The ______________ appreciates the confidence you have shown in choosing us to provide for your health care needs. The service you have elected to participate in implies a financial responsibility on your part. The responsibility obligates you to ensure payment in full of our fees. As a courtesy, we will verify your coverage and bill your insurance carrier on your behalf. However, you are ultimately responsible for payment of your bill.

You are responsible for payment of any deductible and co-payment/co-insurance as determined by your contract with your insurance carrier. We expect these payments at the time of service. Many insurance companies have additional stipulations that may affect your coverage. You are responsible for any amounts not covered by your insurer. If your insurance carrier denies any part of your claim, or if you or your physician elects to continue past your approved period, you will be responsible for your balance in full.

I have read the above policy regarding my financial responsibility to ______________ for providing rehabilitative services to me or the above-named patient. I certify that the information is, to the best of my knowledge, true and accurate. I authorize my insurer to pay any benefits directly to ______________, the full and entire amount of bills incurred by me or the above-named patient, or, if applicable, any amount due after payment has been made by my insurance carrier.

Patient Signature ______________________________ Date ____________

Guarantor Signature ______________________________ Date ____________
(If guarantor is not the patient)

Figure 1-3. Sample financial policy statement (*continues*)

Co-Pay Policy

Some health insurance carriers require the patient to pay a co-pay for services rendered. It is expected and appreciated at the time the service is rendered for the patients to pay at EACH VISIT. Thank you for your cooperation in this matter.

Patient/Guarantor Signature ________________________________ Date ____________________

Consent for Treatment and Authorization to Release Information

I hereby authorize ____________________, through its appropriate personnel, to perform or have performed upon me, or the above named patient, appropriate assessment and treatment procedures.

I further authorize ______________________ to release to appropriate agencies any information acquired in the course of my or the above named patient's examination and treatment.

Patient/Guarantor Signature ________________________________ Date ____________________

Cancellation/No Show Policy

We understand there may be times when you miss an appointment due to an emergency or obligation to work or family. However, we urge you to call 24 hours prior to canceling your appointment.

I understand if I no show for two consecutive appointments, no show for three appointments, or cancel a total of four appointments, I may be discharged from care.

The ________________ will notify you in writing, via certified mail, if you are discharged from care.

I have read and understand the above information, and I agree to the terms described:

Patient/Guarantor Signature ________________________________ Date ____________________

Self-Pay

I do not have health insurance and will be responsible for services rendered here at ________________. I agree to pay __________________ the full and entire amount for treatment given to me or to the above-named patient at each visit.

Patient/Guarantor Signature ________________________________ Date ____________________

Late Fee/Interest Charges

There will be a monthly interest rate of 6 percent added to the balance-due amount of all outstanding patient bills due after the 90th day of the first patient statement that is sent.

Patient/Guarantor Signature ________________________________ Date ____________________

Acceptable Forms of Payment

Our office accepts cash, personal checks, and credit/debit cards.

Figure 1-3. Sample financial policy statement

THE NEXT STEP IN THE COLLECTIONS PROCESS

Once a patient has been seen in the medical office, a document listing the patient's services, procedures, and diagnoses, known as a **health insurance claim** on a CMS-1500 form, is submitted to the patient's health insurance company for physician reimbursement (see Figure 1-4). Once a claim has been submitted, it begins to **age**, or grow old. This aging process of claims is one of two reasons why collections exist; the other is collecting money due from patients. The combined monies due the medical practice from both insurance companies and patients make up the practice's **accounts receivable**.

THE ROLE OF THE COLLECTIONS CLERK

Because accounts receivable will always exist in the medical office, the ongoing process of collecting may be assigned to a **collections clerk**, the person responsible for this job. Duties of a collections clerk may include:

- Telephone calls to patients
- Telephone calls to insurance companies
- Mailing patient due bills
- Writing **appeal letters** (letters submitted to insurance companies requesting reconsideration of payment on a denied claim)
- Filing complaints with the **state insurance commissioner** (the appointed official in charge of each state's Department of Insurance)

THE ROLE OF CUSTOMER SERVICE IN COLLECTIONS

Customer service, the provision of service to customers (patients) before, during, and after a purchase (service), is an integral part of both in-home and **outsourced** (sending work off-site) collections.

Customer service in the medical office is an ongoing process. Unlike a retail store, where the customer may make only one purchase, the customer (patient) in a medical office has a continuous relationship with the provider of service. If there is a breakdown in customer service when collecting, the patient may choose to terminate the relationship with the medical office.

1500

HEALTH INSURANCE CLAIM FORM

INSTRUCTIONAL FORM ONLY - NOT APPROVED FOR USE

PICA — PICA — CARRIER

1. MEDICARE (Medicare #)	MEDICAID (Medicaid #)	TRICARE CHAMPUS (Sponsor's SSN)	CHAMPVA (Member ID#)	GROUP HEALTH PLAN (SSN or ID) X	FECA BLK LUNG (SSN)	OTHER (ID)	1a. INSURED'S I.D. NUMBER (For Program in Item 1): 723Z92660

Patient		Insured
2. PATIENT'S NAME (Last Name, First Name, Middle Initial): ADAMS, ANNE	3. PATIENT'S BIRTH DATE MM DD YY: 04 12 1972; SEX M ☐ F X	4. INSURED'S NAME (Last Name, First Name, Middle Initial): SAME
5. PATIENT'S ADDRESS (No., Street): 111 RAIL ROAD	6. PATIENT'S RELATIONSHIP TO INSURED: Self ☐ Spouse ☐ Child ☐ Other ☐	7. INSURED'S ADDRESS (No., Street): SAME
CITY: BRICK; STATE: NJ	8. PATIENT STATUS: Single X Married ☐ Other ☐	CITY; STATE
ZIP CODE: 08724; TELEPHONE (Include Area Code): (732)000 1111	Employed X Full-Time Student ☐ Part-Time Student ☐	ZIP CODE; TELEPHONE (Include Area Code): ( )
9. OTHER INSURED'S NAME (Last Name, First Name, Middle Initial)	10. IS PATIENT'S CONDITION RELATED TO:	11. INSURED'S POLICY GROUP OR FECA NUMBER
a. OTHER INSURED'S POLICY OR GROUP NUMBER	a. EMPLOYMENT? (Current or Previous) ☐ YES X NO	a. INSURED'S DATE OF BIRTH MM DD YY; SEX M ☐ F ☐
b. OTHER INSURED'S DATE OF BIRTH MM DD YY; SEX M ☐ F ☐	b. AUTO ACCIDENT? ☐ YES X NO; PLACE (State)	b. EMPLOYER'S NAME OR SCHOOL NAME: GROCERIES R US
c. EMPLOYER'S NAME OR SCHOOL NAME	c. OTHER ACCIDENT? ☐ YES X NO	c. INSURANCE PLAN NAME OR PROGRAM NAME
d. INSURANCE PLAN NAME OR PROGRAM NAME	10d. RESERVED FOR LOCAL USE	d. IS THERE ANOTHER HEALTH BENEFIT PLAN? ☐ YES X NO If yes, return to and complete item 9 a-d.

READ BACK OF FORM BEFORE COMPLETING & SIGNING THIS FORM.

12. PATIENT'S OR AUTHORIZED PERSON'S SIGNATURE I authorize the release of any medical or other information necessary to process this claim. I also request payment of government benefits either to myself or to the party who accepts assignment below.

SIGNED SOF DATE 0401YYYY

13. INSURED'S OR AUTHORIZED PERSON'S SIGNATURE I authorize payment of medical benefits to the undersigned physician or supplier for services described below.

SIGNED SOF

PATIENT AND INSURED INFORMATION

14. DATE OF CURRENT: MM DD YY — ILLNESS (First symptom) OR INJURY (Accident) OR PREGNANCY (LMP)	15. IF PATIENT HAS HAD SAME OR SIMILAR ILLNESS, GIVE FIRST DATE MM DD YY
16. DATES PATIENT UNABLE TO WORK IN CURRENT OCCUPATION FROM MM DD YY TO MM DD YY	
17. NAME OF REFERRING PROVIDER OR OTHER SOURCE	17a. 17b. NPI
18. HOSPITALIZATION DATES RELATED TO CURRENT SERVICES FROM MM DD YY TO MM DD YY	
19. RESERVED FOR LOCAL USE	20. OUTSIDE LAB? ☐ YES X NO; $ CHARGES
21. DIAGNOSIS OR NATURE OF ILLNESS OR INJURY (Relate Items 1, 2, 3 or 4 to Item 24E by Line) 1. 784 0 2. 3. 4.	22. MEDICAID RESUBMISSION CODE; ORIGINAL REF. NO.
	23. PRIOR AUTHORIZATION NUMBER

	24. A. DATE(S) OF SERVICE From MM DD YY	To MM DD YY	B. PLACE OF SERVICE	C. EMG	D. PROCEDURES, SERVICES, OR SUPPLIES (Explain Unusual Circumstances) CPT/HCPCS	MODIFIER	E. DIAGNOSIS POINTER	F. $ CHARGES	G. DAYS OR UNITS	H. EPSDT Family Plan	I. ID. QUAL.	J. RENDERING PROVIDER ID. #
1	04 01 YY	04 01 YY	11		99202		1	75 00	1		NPI	
2											NPI	
3											NPI	
4											NPI	
5											NPI	
6											NPI	

PHYSICIAN OR SUPPLIER INFORMATION

25. FEDERAL TAX I.D. NUMBER: 112345678; SSN ☐ EIN X	26. PATIENT'S ACCOUNT NO.: ADAAN000	27. ACCEPT ASSIGNMENT? (For govt. claims, see back) X YES ☐ NO	28. TOTAL CHARGE $ 75 00	29. AMOUNT PAID $ 0 00	30. BALANCE DUE $ 75 00
31. SIGNATURE OF PHYSICIAN OR SUPPLIER INCLUDING DEGREES OR CREDENTIALS (I certify that the statements on the reverse apply to this bill and are made a part thereof.) MICHAEL ROWE MD; SIGNED DATE 0402YY	32. SERVICE FACILITY LOCATION INFORMATION: MICHAEL ROWE MD, 123 APPLE LANE, BRICK NJ 08723; a. 9933993399 b.		33. BILLING PROVIDER INFO & PH # (732)222-3333: MICHAEL ROWE MD, 123 APPLE LANE, BRICK NJ 08723; a. 9933993399 b.		

NUCC Instruction Manual available at: www.nucc.org INSTRUCTIONAL USE ONLY - NOT APPROVED FOR USE

Figure 1-4. Sample health insurance claim on a CMS-1500 form

Effective Communications

Both verbal and nonverbal means of communicating with patients are an important aspect of customer service regarding collections. Examples of effective communications are:

- Assist patients with answers regarding their bills/claims
- Assist patients with the appeal process, a process used to request reconsideration of a previously denied claim by the insurance company

Examples of effective nonverbal communications are:

- Providing clear guidelines in the medical office's financial policy statement regarding missed appointment/no-show fees and interest or late charges on overdue bills
- Displaying signs at the front desk and/or in the patient waiting area regarding the medical office's policy on collecting co-payments
- Sending out patient due statements on a monthly basis
- Submit patient refunds on a timely basis

IMPLEMENTING A PLAN

It is imperative for all employees of the medical staff to be aware of the physician's expectations regarding customer service for the patients of the practice. Implementing a plan for customer service might include a customer service training video for new employees and monthly meetings for the staff to discuss concerns, problems, and future goals for the medical office.

CHAPTER SUMMARY

- The collections process begins when the patient calls to schedule an appointment.
- Obtaining the patient's health insurance information prior to the scheduled appointment enables medical office staff to verify coverage.
- Because self-pays are required to pay, the collections process should begin and end on the day of the office visit.
- A fully completed patient registration form is an asset in collecting money from patients, should the need arise.
- Establishing a financial policy for both patient and medical staff awareness of the practice's rules regarding payments is a main tool used to assist in the collections process.
- The patient registration form, a copy of the health insurance card, and a signed financial policy statement should be placed in the patient's medical chart.
- After the patient is seen in the office, the collections process continues with claims submission.

- Although more than one member of the medical staff is responsible for the collections process as a whole, the specific duties following a claim submission may be assigned to a collections clerk.
- Both verbal and non-verbal communications are important aspects of customer service for both in-house and outsourced collections. Customer service is an important aspect for both in-house and outsourced collections.
- Medical offices should implement a plan to ensure all staff members are aware of customer service expectations.

REVIEW QUESTIONS

Multiple choice: Pick the best answer to each question.

1. The collections process begins ________________.
   A. when the patient is seen in the office
   B. when the patient's health insurance claim is submitted
   C. when the patient calls to schedule an appointment
   D. when the patient is sent a bill

2. A person with no health insurance is called a/an ________________.
   A. self-referral
   B. self-pay
   C. self-serve
   D. none of the above

3. A new patient is defined as one who has never been seen before, or who has not been seen in the past ________________.
   A. 24 months
   B. 30 months
   C. 36 months
   D. 48 months

4. Authorization given for payment to be made directly to the provider is called ________________.
   A. assignment of benefits
   B. accepting assignment
   C. direct assignment
   D. assignment of authorization

Fill in the blank: Complete each statement in the space provided.

5. The person who "carries" the health insurance is called the ______________________________.

6. A percentage amount the patient is responsible to pay for the cost of medical services is called ______________________________.

7. The flat fee a patient pays each time for medical services is called a/an ______________________________.

8. The dollar amount the patient must pay out-of-pocket before any reimbursement is made by the insurance company is called the ______________________.

9. The person financially responsible for the patient's account is called the ______________________.

Short answer: Answer each question with a short statement.

10. List nine items that may be found on the health insurance identification card.

11. What is the importance of obtaining health insurance information prior to the patient's scheduled appointment?

12. What can be a result of leaving contact information off of the patient registration form?

13. List eight items that should be included in the medical practice's financial policy.

14. List six means of effective communications for customer service regarding patients.

15. List two ideas that might be included in a customer service plan for the medical office.

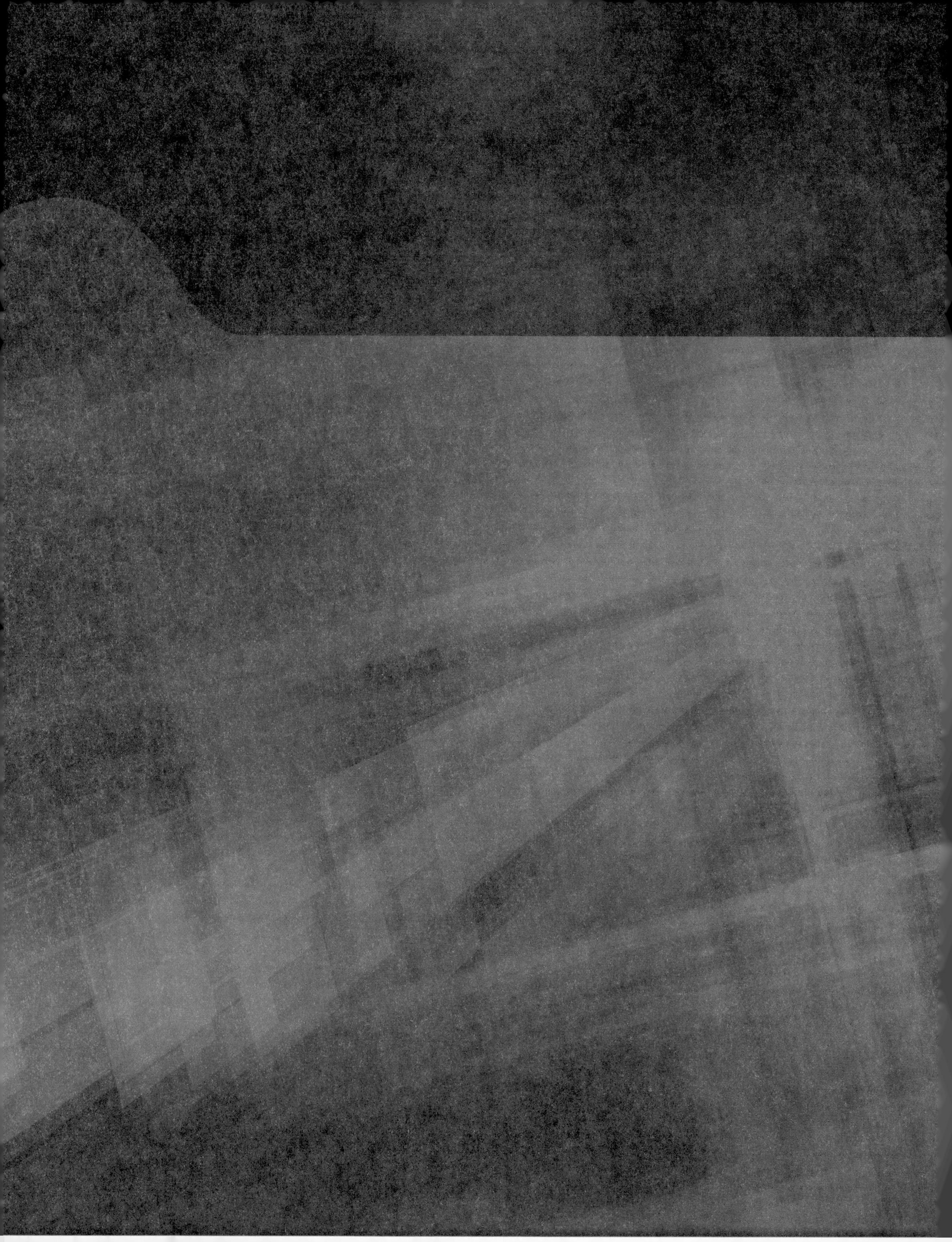

Chapter 2

Legal Guidelines for Collecting

OBJECTIVES

Upon completion of this chapter, the student should be able to:

- Understand federal and state regulations regarding collection practices.
- Discuss frequently asked questions and answers regarding collection practices.
- Describe prohibited collection actions against the patient.
- Define key terms.

KEY TERMS

Collection agencies

Fair Debt Collection Practices Act (FDCPA)

Federal Reserve Board

Federal Reserve System

Health Insurance Portability and Accountability Act of 1996 (HIPAA)

MEDICAL DEBT

In a recent study conducted by the Federal Reserve Board, the governing body of the central banking system (Federal Reserve System) of the United States, it was noted that nearly one-half of collection actions and credit reporting are for debt of unpaid medical bills.

STOP AND ANALYZE

Do you think patients treat medical bills as seriously as other bills; for example, utilities, car payments, or credit cards? Why or why not?

FEDERAL AND STATE REGULATIONS

Guidelines for debt collecting generally apply to collection agencies (agencies retained for the purpose of collecting debts). These guidelines can be found in the Fair Debt Collections Practices Act (FDCPA), the primary United States federal law governing debt collection practices. Although the FDCPA pertains to all states, the act stipulates that if a state law is more restrictive than the federal law, the state law will supersede the federal portion of the act.

NOTE

For Workers' Compensation and No-fault claims, refer to state and federal guidelines regarding balance billing and collection practices. For the purpose of this text, the term 'you' as in 'consumer' referred to in the FDCPA has been changed to 'patient' because the patient is the consumer in the medical office.

FREQUENTLY ASKED QUESTIONS FOR COLLECTION PRACTICES

Although other federal or state laws may apply specifically to in-house collections, the following answers to frequently asked questions may be found in the FDCPA.

Q: *How may I contact a patient?*

A: By mail, telephone, telegram, or facsimile.

Q: *At what hours can I contact the patient?*

A: Not before 8:00 A.M. or after 9:00 P.M., unless the patient agrees.

Q: *May I contact the patient at work?*

A: Yes, unless the patient asks you not to (for example, if the patient's employer disapproves of personal telephone calls).

Q: *May I contact third parties about the patient's debt?*

A: You may contact third parties, but *only* in regard to where the patient resides, the patient's telephone number, and the patient's employer.

Q: *What medical information may I disclose about a patient to a credit reporting agency?*

A: Under Health Insurance Portability and Accountability Act of 1996 (HIPAA) laws, those stipulating patients' privacy rights regarding their protected health information, you may disclose *only* the following:

- Name and address
- Date of birth
- Social Security number
- Payment history
- Account number
- Name and address of the one claiming the debt

Q: *Can a medical office charge interest on overdue bills?*

A: Yes; however, the amount of interest the office adds to overdue bills must be listed in the office's financial policy statement.

NOTE

The legal amount of interest varies by state and should be investigated further by the medical office collecting on the debt.

PROHIBITED PRACTICES

Under the FDCPA, debt collectors may not harass, abuse, or oppress the patient.

For example, debt collectors may not do the following:

- Use threats of violence or harm.
- Publish a list of patients who refuse to pay their debts (except to a credit bureau).
- Use obscene or profane language, or repeatedly use the telephone to annoy someone.
- Give false credit information about the patient to anyone, including a credit bureau.
- Send the patient anything that looks like an official document from a court or government agency when it is not.

- Use a false name.
- Collect any amount greater than the debt unless state law permits such a charge.
- Deposit a post-dated check prematurely.
- Use deception to make the patient accept collect calls or pay for telegrams.
- Take or threaten to take the patient's property unless this can be done legally.
- Contact the patient by postcard.

Debt collectors may not use false or misleading statements when collecting a debt. For example, debt collectors may not:

- Falsely imply that they are attorneys or government representatives.
- Falsely imply that the patient has committed a crime.
- Falsely represent that they operate or work for a credit bureau.
- Misrepresent the amount of the patient's debt.
- Indicate that the papers being sent to the patient are legal forms when they are not.
- Indicate that the papers being sent to the patient are not legal forms when they are.

Debt collectors also may not state to the patient that:

- The patient will be arrested if the debt is not paid.
- They (the debt collector) will seize, garnish, attach, or sell property or wages, unless they intend to do so and it is legal to do so.
- Actions, such as lawsuits, will be taken against the patient when such action legally may not be taken, or when they do not intend to take such action.

STOP AND ANALYZE

Have you or someone you've known been the victim of harassment or abuse by a debt collector? How did it make you/the person feel?

CHAPTER SUMMARY

- Findings resulting from a study conducted by the Federal Reserve Board reported that nearly one-half of collection actions and credit reporting was debt of unpaid medical bills.
- The FDCPA contains laws governing debt collection practices.
- Although the FDCPA pertains to all states, state law supersedes federal law if the state law is more restrictive.
- HIPAA laws stipulate patients' privacy rights regarding their protected health information.
- The FDCPA prohibits against harassing, abusing, and oppressing the patient.

REVIEW QUESTIONS

Multiple choice: Pick the best answer to each question.

1. Debt for unpaid medical bills represents ________________ of collections actions and credit reporting.
   A. one-third
   B. one-half
   C. one-quarter
   D. two-thirds

2. The central banking system of the United States is known as ________________.
   A. Federal Reserve System
   B. Federal Banking System
   C. Federal Regulatory System
   D. Federal Reserve Board

3. At what hours can a patient be contacted?
   A. Between 8:00 A.M. and 8:00 P.M.
   B. Not before 8:00 A.M. or after 9:00 P.M.
   C. Not before 7:00 A.M. or after 9:00 P.M.
   D. Not before 8:00 A.M. or after 10:00 P.M.

Short answer: Answer each question with a short statement.

4. Under HIPAA laws, what information regarding the patient may be disclosed?

____

____

____

____

____

5. If a medical office intends to charge interest on overdue bills, where should this be listed?

____

____

____

____

____

6. List three prohibited practices by debt collectors.

7. List three prohibited false or misleading statements by debt collectors.

Chapter 3

Aging Reports and the Department of Insurance

OBJECTIVES

Upon completion of this chapter, the student should be able to:

- Understand a claim's aging process.
- Decipher the insurance aging report and the patient aging report.
- Explain the importance of maintaining accounts receivable.
- Understand the role of the state insurance commissioner regarding medical collections.
- Explain necessary documentation needed to accompany a complaint.
- Describe potential outcomes of complaints against insurance companies.
- Define key terms.

KEY TERMS

Cash flow
Clean claim
Department of Insurance
Electronic claims
Following-up
Insurance aging report
Maintaining
NPI (National Provider Identifier)
Outstanding
Paper claims
Patient aging report
Payers
Prompt payment statutes
Re-billing
State insurance commissioner
Uninsured

THE AGING PROCESS

Once a health insurance claim is submitted, it begins to age (see Figure 3-1). State laws vary with regard to **prompt payment statutes**, which are guidelines for timely payment of a health insurance claim. There are also differences for payment of **electronic claims** (those submitted via a computer modem) and **paper claims** (those printed and sent by mail). Many states refer to **clean claims** (those with no errors) in regards to the prompt payment laws. See Table 3-1.

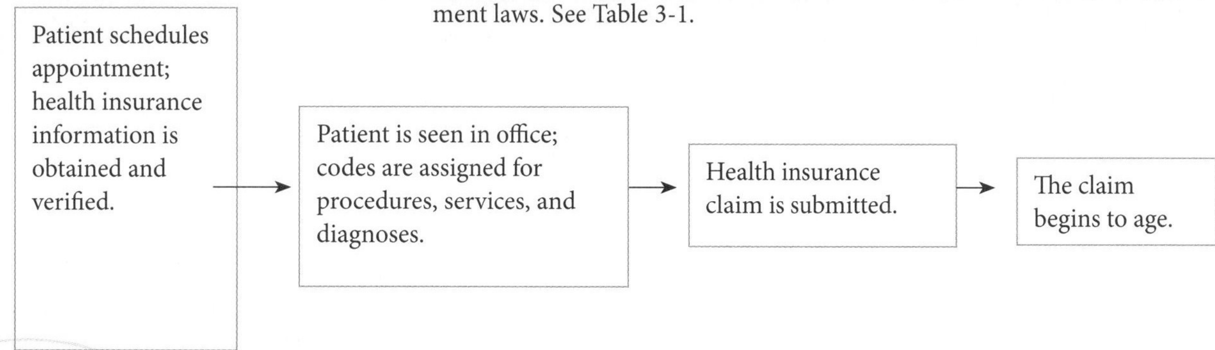

Figure 3-1. The beginning of the aging process

Table 3-1. "Prompt Pay" Statutes and Regulations

State	Status/Terms of Law
Alabama	Clean claims paid within 45 working days; applies to HMOs only.
Alaska	Clean claims must be paid within 30 working days.
Arizona	Clean claims must be paid within 30 days or interest payments are required (usually about 10%).
Arkansas	Clean, electronic claims must be paid or denied in 30 calendar days; paper claims in 45. 12% per annum interest after 60 days.
California	Claims must be paid within 45 working days for an HMO; 30 days for other health service plans. Interest accrues at 15% per annum or $15 penalty, whichever is greater.
Colorado	Claims must be paid in 30 calendar days if submitted electronically; 45 days if paper claims. 10% annual interest penalty.
Connecticut	Claims must be paid within 45 days. Interest accrues at 15% per annum.
Delaware	Clean claims must be paid in 30 days.
District of Columbia	Clean claims will be paid in 30 days. Interest payable at 1.5% days 31–60; 2% days 61–120; and 2.5% after 120 days. Applies to claims received on or after October 16, 2002.

Table 3-1. "Prompt Pay" Statutes and Regulations *(continued)*

State	Status/Terms of Law
Florida	Clean HMO claims (paper or electronic) must be paid in 35 days; non-HMO in 45 days. Claims where information was requested must be paid in 120 days. Interest penalty is 10% per year. Statute # 31555.
Georgia	Claims must be paid within 15 working days. Interest accrues at 18% per annum.
Hawaii	Clean, paper claims must be paid in 30 days; electronic claims within 15 days. Interest accrues at 15% per annum. Commissioner may impose fines.
Idaho	Paper claims settled in 45 days; electronic claims in 30 days. Chapter 56.
Illinois	Clean claims must be paid in 30 days. Interest accrues at 9% per annum.
Indiana	Paper claims must be paid in 45 days; electronic claims must be paid in 30 days.
Iowa	Payment to be made in 30 days. Penalty is 10% per annum.
Kansas	Claims will be paid in 30 days. Interest accrues at a rate of 1% per month.
Kentucky	Claims must be paid or denied within 30 calendar days. Interest accrues at 12% per annum when 31-60 days late; 18% when 61–90 days late; and 21% when 91+ days late.
Louisiana	Claims submitted electronically must be paid within 25 days. If not paid within 25 days, the health insurance issuer shall pay to the claimant an additional late payment adjustment equal to 1% of the unpaid balance due for each month.
Maine	Clean claims must be paid within 30 days. Interest accrues at 1.5% per month.
Maryland	Clean claims must be paid within 30 days. Interest accrues at monthly rates of 1.5% when 31–60 days late; 2% when 61–120 days late), and 2.5% when 121+ days late, respectively.
Massachusetts	MCL 500.2006 MCL 200.111
Michigan	A clean claim submitted to an insurance company with all the correct information shall be paid within 45 days. Penalty is 12% interest. The laws also hold Medicaid and HMOs to this 45-day schedule.
Minnesota	Clean claims must be paid in 30 days. Interest accrues at 1.5% per month if not paid or denied.
Mississippi	Clean claims must be paid within 25 days if electronic; 35 days if paper claim. Interest accrues at 1.5% per month.

(continues)

Table 3-1. "Prompt Pay" Statutes and Regulations *(continued)*

State	Status/Terms of Law
Missouri	Claims must be acknowledged within 10 days and paid or denied within 15 days of receipt of requested additional information. Interest penalty of 1% per month applies to claims not paid within 45 days. After 40 processing days, the provider is entitled to a per day penalty: 50% of claim (up to $20) if they notify the carrier. This penalty will accrue for 30 days only, unless the provider served notice again. Rules also stipulate that re-contracted providers may file claims up to one year from the date of service; contracted providers for six months unless the contract states otherwise. Refunds cannot be requested after 12 months.
Montana	Clean claims must be paid within 30 days. Interest accrues at 18% per annum. Montana annotated code 33-18-232.
Nebraska	Claims must be paid or denied within 15 days of affirmation of liability.
Nevada	Claims must be paid in 30 days. Penalty interest accrues at the rate set forth in Nevada Revised Statute 99.040.
New Hampshire	Effective January 1, 2001, clean paper claims must be paid in 45 days, electronic claims in 15 days. There is a 1.5% monthly interest penalty.
New Jersey	Clean, electronic claims must be paid within 30 days, paper claims within 40 days.
New Mexico	Clean claims must be paid within 30 days if electronic; 45 days if paper. Interest accrues at 1½ % per month.
New York	Claims must be paid within 45 days. Interest accrues at greater of 12% per year or corporate tax rate determined by Commissioner. Fines up to $500 per day possible.
North Carolina	Claims must be paid or denied within 30 days. Annual interest penalty of 18%.
North Dakota	Claims must be paid within 15 days.
Ohio	Payer must notify provider within 15 days of receipt if claim is materially deficient; payer must process claims in 30 days if no supporting documentation is needed. If payer requests additional information, this must be done within 30 days of receipt of claim. Claim must be processed in 45 days from receipt of requested information.
Oklahoma	Clean claims must be paid within 45 days. Penalty of 10% of claim as interest for late claims.
Oregon	Effective January 1, 2002, clean claims must be paid in 30 days. A 12% interest penalty applies.
Pennsylvania	Clean claims must be paid in 45 days. Provider must be licensed in Pennsylvania.
Rhode Island	Written claims to be paid in 40 calendar days, electronic in 30 days.

(continues)

Table 3-1. "Prompt Pay" Statutes and Regulations *(continued)*

State	Status/Terms of Law
South Carolina	Group health insurers must pay claims in 60 days.
South Dakota	Electronic claims must be paid in 30 days, paper claims in 45 days.
Tennessee	Clean, commercial claims sent electronically must be paid within 21 days, paper claims in 30 days. Interest accrues at 1% per month.
Texas	Effective September 1, 2003, paper claims to be paid in 45 days and electronic claims in 30 days. Interest accrues at 18%.
Utah	Effective September 1, 2001, claims must be paid or denied in 30 days. Penalty interest may be applied to formula.
Vermont	Claims must be paid or denied in 45 days. Interest penalty is 12% per annum.
Virginia	Clean claims must be paid within 40 days.
Washington	95% of the monthly volume of clean claims shall be paid in 30 days. 95% of the monthly volume of all claims shall be paid or denied within 60 days.
West Virginia	Claims must be paid in 30 days if electronic, 40 days if paper. Interest and fines may apply. Interest penalty of 10% per annum.
Wisconsin	If clean claims are not paid within 30 days, they are subject to a penalty interest rate of 12% per year.
Wyoming	Claims must be paid within 45 days. Penalties and fines may accrue.

INSURANCE AGING REPORTS

Health insurance claims that have not yet been paid or denied are called **outstanding**. A list of these claim balances by **payers** (insurance companies) is called the **insurance aging report**.

Although medical practice software programs vary by office, most insurance aging reports (see Figure 3-2) will consist of the following:

- Name of the payer
- Name and account number of the patient
- The health insurance identification number of the patient
- Dates of service for all outstanding claims
- Columns showing the age of each claim
- The total amount due the provider from each payer

Date of Service	Procedure	Age of claim by days 0–30	Age of claim by days 31–60	Age of claim by days 61–90	Age of claim by days 91–120	Age of claim by days 120+	Total Balance
Aetna							Aetna Total $175.00
Ablal 001 Ables, Allison 06-01-XX	99214	$75.00					$75.00
Andag 001 Anders, Agnes 03-05-XX	99203			$100			$100.00
Blue Cross Blue Shield							BC/BS Total $280.00
Bonbe 001 Bones, Betty 01-03-XX	99213 81002					$50.00 $25.00	$75.00
Bulbo 001 Bully, Bonnie 05-10-XX	99204 69210		$125.00 0 $80.00				$205.00
Cigna							Cigna Total $175.00
Culco 001 Cullen, Colleen 06-05-XX	99215	$100.00 0					$100.00
Czeca 001 Czey, Cathy 05-11-XX	99202		$75.00				$75.00
Healthnet							Healthnet Total $210.00
Harhe 001 Harvey, Henry 12-15-XX	99205					$150.00	$150.00
Hulho 001 Hulk, Howard 04-27-XX	36415 81002		$35.00 $25.00				$60.00
Medicare							Medicare Total $245.00
Meama 001 Mears, Marvin 03-07-XX	99212				$45.00		$45.00
Mulma 001 Muller, Mary 04-01-XX	20610			$200.00 0			$200.00

Figure 3-2. Sample insurance aging report

FOLLOW-UP

When medical office personnel call a payer to check the status of an outstanding claim, this is known as **following-up** on the claim. This function is an extremely important aspect in **maintaining**, or keeping current, the office's accounts receivable. The process of following-up begins with printing the insurance aging report. The next sections provide examples of follow-up techniques.

Using the Internet

Several payers allow providers to check the status of a claim on the payer's website via the Internet. Although this may be a quick and easy way for following-up, it can be frustrating as well. Because the person following-up on a claim cannot ask the computer a question, a call to the payer may be required if additional information about the status of the claim is needed.

STOP AND PRACTICE

Exercise 3-1

Refer to Figure 3-2 to answer the following.

1. What is Allison Ables' account number?

   ____

2. What is the procedure code for Colleen Cullen's claim?

   ____

3. What is the date of service for Henry Harvey's claim?

   ____

4. What is the total balance due for Howard Hulk's claim?

   ____

5. How many claims are outstanding in the 0–30-days-old column?

   ____

6. Which payer has the highest outstanding claim balance?

   ____

Telephone Calls

When making telephone calls as the follow-up method, be prepared to have the following information on hand:

- Provider's National Provider Identifier (NPI) (a 10-digit number identifying the provider to the payer)
- Insured's health identification number
- Patient's name
- Patient's date of birth
- Date of service
- Dollar amount of claim

After searching the payer's computerized software system, the customer service representative may give one of several reasons why a claim has not yet been paid. These reasons can include:

- No record of claim on file
- The claim is in process
- Payment has been delayed pending receipt of additional information requested from the provider (i.e. progress notes)
- Payment has been delayed pending receipt of additional information requested from the patient (i.e. a coordination of benefits form which requests information about a possible additional health insurance plan the patient may have)

Table 3-2 lists the suggested course of action medical office personnel can take to assist in payment of the claim.

Table 3-2. Suggested courses of action for medical office personnel

Reason for delay	Suggested course of action
No record of claim on file.	If claim was submitted electronically, give the customer service representative the confirmation number from the Electronic Data Interchange (EDI) report. If the claim still cannot be located, re-submit the claim, or ask if the claim can be faxed, and have the customer service representative call to confirm it was received.
The claim is in process	If the payer has exceeded the prompt payment guidelines for that state, remind payer of this and inform payer that a complaint will be filed with the state insurance commissioner if payment is not received in two weeks.
Payment delayed pending receipt of additional information requested from the provider.	Ask the customer service representative specifically what is needed to process the claim and fax the request immediately. Request confirmation of receipt.
Payment delayed pending receipt of additional information requested from the patient	Call and ask the patient to send the response promptly, so that the provider can be paid. Inform the patient that the balance of the claim may be transferred to the patient if the request is not received.

Re-billing

The process of re-submitting an outstanding claim is called re-billing. Rules regarding the re-billing of claims that have not yet been followed-up vary amongst offices. Some offices may re-bill all outstanding claims after 30 days; others may wait 60 days.

REGULATING INSURANCE COMPANIES

Every insurance company that offers health insurance must be licensed with the Department of Insurance, the governmental agency in charge of controlling and regulating insurance companies.

The appointed official in charge of each state's Department of Insurance is known as the state insurance commissioner (Appendix II provides a table that lists each state's Department of Insurance contact information).

Complaints

When an insurance company delays payments of medical claims and ignores repeated claim inquiries, the provider may choose to file a complaint with the state insurance commissioner against such insurance company.

These complaints may be made online (if able) or by mail using the appropriate Department of Insurance form (see Figure 3-3). If the Department of Insurance has a specific complaint form to complete, the provider should use that form. The complaint should include:

- Copy of the claim(s) in question
- Printout from the patient's account of all documented inquiries to and correspondence with the insurance company in question

If a state's Department of Insurance does not have a specific complaint form, the medical office may create its own like the sample shown in Figure 3-4.

Potential outcomes for complaints could include:

- Payment of claim(s) in question
- Financial penalty for the insurance company
- Loss of license to practice insurance in that state

See Figure 3-5.

When reimbursement for claims is a direct result of a filed complaint, it is easy to understand why the state insurance commissioner plays such an important role in medical office collections.

INSURANCE COMPLAINT FORM Office of the Commissioner of Insurance

The Office of the Commissioner of Insurance assists consumers with their insurance problems. In order for us to investigate your complaint, please complete this form as thoroughly as you can and return it to us at the address shown above. A copy of your complaint will be sent to the company or agent with a request to respond directly to you and to advise our office of the action taken. You should hear from the company or agent in about 25 days from the date you send us your complaint. When we receive the information from the company or agent, we will review the file to determine what action we can take. We will notify you of our determination. If our office is unable to obtain the resolution you desired, you may consider contacting a private attorney for advice. If your complaint involved a claim dispute, you may want to contact your county's small claims court.

TYPE OR PRINT CLEARLY WITH A BLACK PEN. COMPLETE BOTH SIDES OF THIS FORM.

1. Your Name ____________________
   Mailing Address ____________________
   City __________ State __________ Zip Code __________
   Phone number where we can reach you between 8:00 - 4:30 p.m. __________

2. Name of Insurance Company Involved
   ____
   (Please provide the PRECISE NAME of the insurance company. Incorrect names will delay the handling of your complaint. The name of the company can be found on your insurance policy, usually on the first page.)

3. I am filing this complaint as:
   ☐ Insured ☐ Agent ☐ Third-Party
   ☐ Provider ☐ Other (specify) __________

4. Type of Insurance
   ☐ Auto ☐ Individual Acc/Health ☐ Business ☐ Life/Annuity
   ☐ Home ☐ Group Acc/Health ☐ Other (specify) __________

5. Name of Insurance Agent Who Sold the Insurance **(Not the same as 2., above)**

6. Name and Address of Insurance Agency, If Applicable **(Not the same as 2., above)**

7. Name of Policyholder (if other than 1., above)	8. Policy or Certificate #
9. Date Policy or Certificate Was Sold	10. State in Which Policy or Certificate Was Sold
11. Claim or File #, If Applicable	12. Date Loss Occurred or Began, If Applicable

Figure 3-3. Sample Department of Insurance Complaint Form (*continues*)

13. Please describe your problem in detail. Attach additional pages, if necessary. Please include **copies** of important papers, letters, or other information, if they relate to your problem.

PLEASE SEND COPIES ONLY—NO ORIGINALS AND NO PHOTOS.

14. Please indicate how you think your problem should be resolved.

15. Have you previously reported this problem to us or any other governmental agency?

☐ Yes ☐ No If yes, state which agency and what action was taken?

Consent to Release Information

The information I have given above is true and accurate to the best of my knowledge and belief. This information may be forwarded to the insurance company and/or agent involved. Any medical information which I have provided, may be shared with the insurance company, if necessary for the investigation of this matter. I understand that under Open Records Law all information which is in my file, including personal and health information, may become a public record once my file is closed. Only actual medical records which are obtained from a health care provider are confidential under state law.

Signature Date

Figure 3-3. Sample Department of Insurance Complaint Form (*continued*)

Practice Name ______________________________ Date ______________

Address ____

City, State, Zip ____

Phone ____

We filed the attached claim form with the (insert name of company) Insurance Company on (insert date). It has not been paid or denied.

Please accept this letter as a formal written complaint against the (insert name of company) Insurance Company.

Figure 3-4. Sample doctor-initiated complaint to a state insurance commissioner

Federal Ruling

A quote from Judge Rafeedie in the federal court case of: Kanne v. Connecticut General Ins. Co., 607 F. Supp. 899 (1985) on upholding $750,000 in additional damages for unreasonable delay in payment of medical claims:

"Repeated requests for payment of the bills were made to the claims representative, and copies of the bills were in the Insurance Company's possession. Under these circumstances, it is not proper for the insurer to sit back and delay payment claims, under the pretextual theory that the Doctors have not dotted all the i's and crossed all the t's. On the contrary, the insurer has the duty to see to it that the promised protection is delivered when needed. It must act to facilitate the claims instead of searching for reasons not to do so."

Figure 3-5. Example of a federal ruling against an insurance company

PATIENT AGING REPORT

A list showing patient due balances owed to the provider is called the **patient aging report**. The dollar amounts shown on this report can represent balances from:

- Deductible amounts
- Co-insurance amounts

- Non-covered services
- Uninsured (patients without health insurance coverage)

A patient aging report, which is similar in appearance to the insurance aging report, should list:

- Columns showing the age, by days, of the patient due balances
- Patient's account number
- Total balance due from the patient

NOTE

Because software programs vary, the patient and insurance aging reports may contain more or less than the samples provided. See Figure 3-6.

Account #	Name	0–30	31–60	61–90	91+	Patient Total Balance
adamad01	Adam Adams	$20.70				$20.70
cohebe01	Betty Cohen				$175.00	$175.00
doejan01	Jane Doe	$7.40		$11.20		$18.60
flocfr03	Freda Flock		$21.60			$21.60
martma01	Martin Martinson		$7.20	$11.20	$6.80	$25.20
smitja10	John Jacob J. Smith	$11.20				$11.20
thomto02	Tom Thomas		$12.30			$12.30
westwa01	Wayne West	$5.60				$5.60
Balances by days		$44.90	$41.10	$22.40	$181.80	

Figure 3-6. Sample patient aging report

STOP AND PRACTICE

Exercise 3-2

Refer to Figure 3-3 to answer the following.

1. What is Jane Doe's account number?

 ____

2. How many patients are in the 31–60-days-old column?

 ____

3. Which patient's balance represents a claim that may have been applied to the patient's deductible, or the patient may be uninsured?

 ____

4. Which column represents the least amount due to the provider?

 ____

Consistency

It is imperative that follow-up be performed on a routine basis. Most offices perform this task monthly. When accounts receivable are worked consistently, there is a greater chance for a steady **cash flow**, a stream of cash (income) used for disbursements.

ROLE PLAYING ACTIVITY

Student A will play the role of the medical office personnel (MOP) calling to check the status of a claim.

Student B will play the role of the customer service representative (CSR) at the insurance company.

See Table 3-3 for role-playing dialogue.

Table 3-3. Dialog for role-playing activity

Scenario	Student A	Student B
Ms. Joan Lewis was seen in the office, has Medicare, and her claim is 60 days old.	"Hi, I am calling to check the status of a claim."	"May I have the provider's NPI?"
	"0000111100."	"May I have the patient's Medicare number?"
	"123456789A."	"What is the date of service in question?"
	"6/30/XX."	

ROLE PLAYING ACTIVITY

Table 3-4 lists different responses from the CSR and the suggested action the medical office personnel might take.

Table 3-4. Responses from the CSR and suggested actions

CSR response	Action by medical office personnel
"That claim was processed and paid on 7/21/XX."	Pull the Medicare Remittance Advice (MRA) for that date. If in fact the payment is listed, post the payment and make any necessary adjustments in the computerized software program.
"I am not showing that identification number as valid."	Pull the patient's chart. Compare the copy of the patient's ID card with the health insurance ID number listed in the patient's account in the computer software program. It may be the ID number was entered incorrectly into the system. If this is the case, correct the ID number and re-bill the claim.
"That claim was processed and applied to the patient's deductible on 7/21/XX."	Pull the MRA for that date and transfer the correct amount to the patient.

ROLE PLAYING ACTIVITY

Think of collection scenarios with your classmates and develop your own dialogue of how you would respond to the situation.

CHAPTER SUMMARY

- A health insurance claim begins to age once it has been submitted to the payer.
- Prompt payment statutes are guidelines for timely payment of claims.
- Electronic claims are sent to the payer via a computer modem and paper claims are printed and mailed to the payer.
- Clean claims are ones with no errors.
- Outstanding claims are those that have not yet been paid or denied.
- Payer is another term for an insurance company.
- The insurance aging report is a list of monies due the physician from payers.
- Although medical office software programs vary, most insurance aging reports will consist of:
    - Name of the payer
    - Name and account number of the patient
    - Dates of service for outstanding claims
    - Columns showing the age of each claim
- Following-up on claims is an important aspect of maintaining the office's accounts receivable.
- Using the Internet and checking a claim's status on the payer's website is one way to perform follow-up.
- Making telephone calls to the payer to check the status of a claim is an additional follow-up method.
- It is important to have the following available when calling a payer to check claim status:
    - Provider's NPI
    - Insured person's health identification number
    - Patient's name
    - Patient's date of birth
    - Date of service
    - Dollar amount of claim
- When given the reason for delayed payment of a claim, the medical office personnel should take the necessary action to assist in payment of the claim.
- Re-billing rules vary between offices and can be done on all outstanding claims prior to following-up or on only the necessary claims needing re-billing to ensure payment.
- The patient aging report is a list of monies due to the provider from patient balances. Figures may represent:
    - Deductible amounts
    - Co-insurance amounts
    - Balances from uninsured patients

- Consistency is important in maintaining both accounts receivable and cash flow
- Insurance companies offering health insurance in a specific state must be licensed with that state's Department of Insurance.
- The state insurance commissioner is the appointed official in charge of each state's Department of Insurance.
- A simple threat to file a complaint with the state insurance commissioner may result in expedited payment of a claim.
- A provider may choose to file a complaint with a state insurance commissioner regarding delayed payments and failure to respond to repeated claim inquiries.
- Each state's Department of Insurance may require the complaint to be completed on a specific form either online or by mail; generic forms may be used if none exist.

REVIEW QUESTIONS

Fill in the blank: Complete each statement in the space provided.

1. Guidelines for timely payment of claims are called ______________________________.

2. Claims submitted via a computer modem are called ______________________________.

3. Claims printed and sent via mail are called ______________________________.

4. A claim with no errors is referred to as a/an ______________________________claim.

5. Claims that have not yet been paid or denied are called ______________________________.

6. Another term for an insurance company is ______________________________.

7. Checking the status of a claim is also known as ______________________________.

8. Keeping the office's accounts receivable current is known as ______________________________.

9. A 10-digit number identifying the provider to the payer is called the ______________________________.

10. A patient with no health insurance is known as ______________________________.

11. A steady stream of cash (income) used for disbursements is called ______________________________.

Multiple choice: Pick the best answer to each question.

12. All of the following should be on hand, except ________________ when calling the payer to check claim status.
    A. patient's name
    B. date of service
    C. dollar amount of claim
    D. patient's salary

13. The process of re-submitting an outstanding claim is called ________________.
    A. re-calculating
    B. re-sending
    C. re-billing
    D. re-figuring

14. A list showing patient-due balances owed to the provider is called ________________.
    A. day sheet
    B. patient aging report
    C. patient ledger
    D. insurance billing worksheet

Short answer: Answer each question with a short statement.

15. At what stage does a claim begin to age?

16. Although software programs vary between offices, list three items found on an insurance aging report.

17. List two methods of follow-up.

18. What role does the Department of Insurance play in collections?

19. What necessary documentation should accompany a complaint?

Define the following key terms.

20. Clean claim

21. Electronic claims

22. Following-up

23. Insurance aging report

24. Maintaining

25. Outstanding

26. Paper claims

27. Patient aging report

____
____
____

28. Payers

____
____
____

29. Prompt payment statutes

____
____
____

30. Re-billing

____
____
____

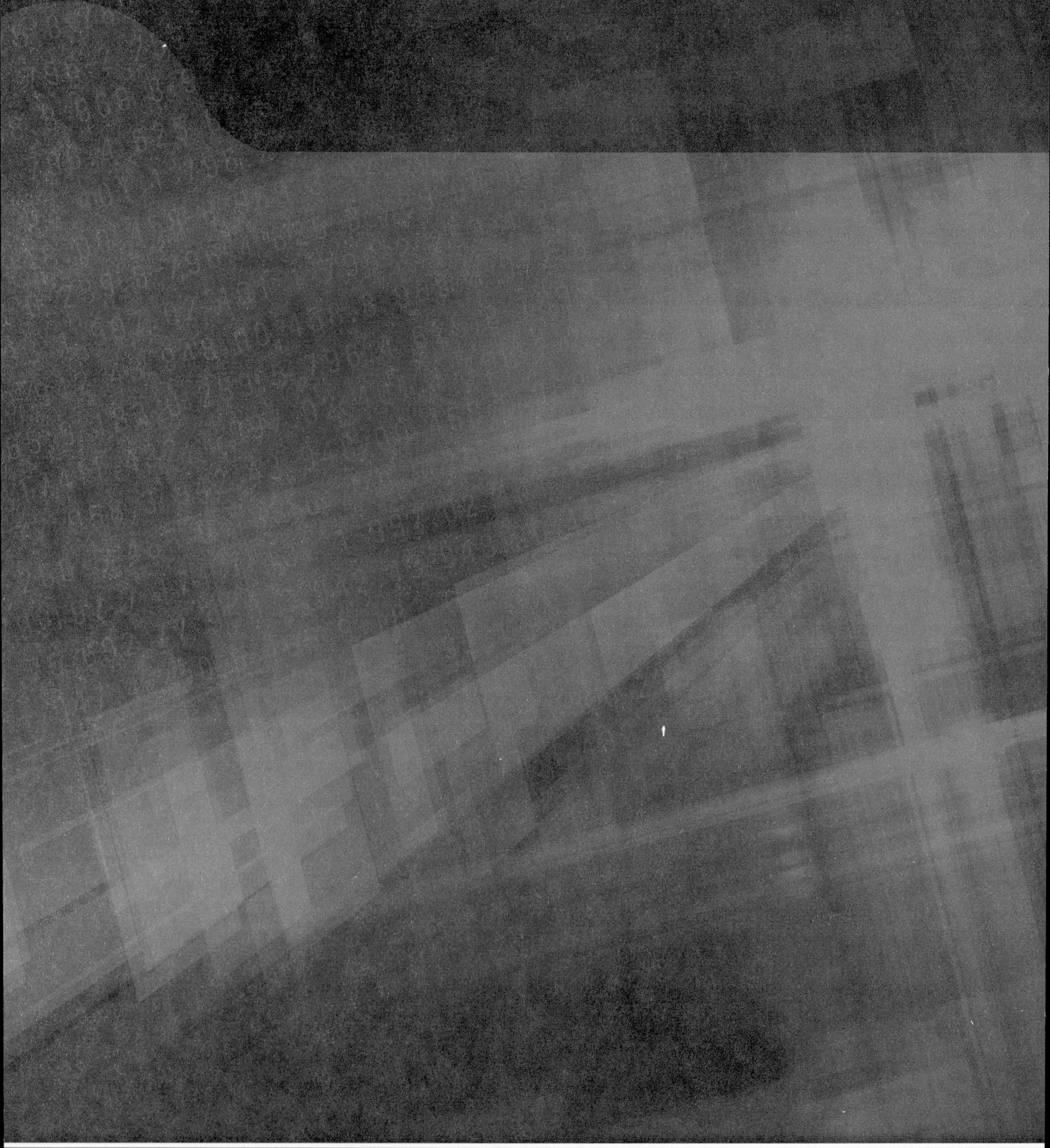

Chapter 4

In-Office Patient Collection Strategies

OBJECTIVES

Upon completion of this chapter, the student should be able to:

- Explain the importance of insurance verification.
- Describe different patient collection strategies.
- Discuss the importance of consistency in patient mailing statements.
- Define key terms.

KEY TERMS

Allowed amount

Fee schedule

Indemnity plan

Managed care plan

Medicare

Patient statement

Payment arrangement

Post-dated check

Superbill

Supplemental plan

Traditional plan

HEALTH INSURANCE VERIFICATION

Verifying patient's health insurance coverage prior to the scheduled appointment is one way to reduce in-office collections. By calling the insurance company to verify what type of plan the patient has, the office is then aware of the patient's responsibility for payment. For example:

- **Indemnity plan** — a type of insurance plan in which reimbursement is made at 80% of the allowed amount. The patient is then responsible to pay the remaining 20%.
- **Managed care plan** — a health insurance plan that includes financing management and delivery of health care services; usually requires a co-payment.

Co-insurance

If the patient has an indemnity plan, also known as a **traditional plan**, the insurance company is usually responsible to pay 80% of the **allowed amount**, the dollar amount an insurance company deems fair for a specific service or procedure. Because the front desk staff of a medical practice does not normally have an indemnity payer's **fee schedule** (a list of allowed amounts for all services and procedures payable by the insurance company), the patient's 20% responsibility is not known until after the health insurance claim has been paid. In this case, a **patient statement** (a bill reflecting the patient's responsibility for payment) can be sent out.

Medicare

Medicare, a government plan in which reimbursement for most services and procedures is paid at 80% of the allowed amount, remains consistent in its payments for all patients belonging to the same practice. A Medicare fee schedule can be obtained from the Medicare Web site for the state in question. Once obtained, a member of the front desk staff can calculate the 20% patient-due portion for each service and the appropriate procedure listed on the office's **superbill** (a form listing CPT, HCPCS, and ICD-9-CM codes used to record services performed for the patient and the patient's diagnosis(es) for a given visit). The completed 'patient due' superbill should be conspicuously posted at the front desk. See Figure 4-1.

This collection strategy is most useful for those Medicare patients not covered by a **supplemental plan**, a secondary insurance plan intended to cover the cost of the patient's deductible and/or 20% co-insurance.

Collecting this 20% patient-due money up-front reduces future collections and aids in maintaining the medical office's accounts receivable.

Co-payment

A co-payment is to be paid at the time services are rendered. Many medical offices have signs posted at the front desk and throughout the waiting room, which state: "*Co-payment must be paid prior to being seen.*"

Office Codes

New Pt	Established Pt	Consult
$\$7^{93}$ 99201	$\$4^{73}$ 99211	$\$10^{86}$ 99241
$\$14^{03}$ 99202	$\$8^{36}$ 99212	$\$19^{76}$ 99242
$\$20^{84}$ 99203	$\$11^{37}$ 99213	$\$26^{35}$ 99243
$\$29^{42}$ 99204	$\$17^{80}$ 99214	$\$37^{10}$ 99244
$\$37^{30}$ 99205	$\$25^{78}$ 99215	$\$47^{92}$ 99245

$\$5^{89}$ 93000 EKG	.91 82270 Hemocult
$0 36415 Venipuncture	.17 J3420 Vitamin B-12 injection
$\$4^{05}$ 90772 Therapeutic injection	$\$1^{05}$ J1030 Depo-Medrol
$\$10^{53}$ 69210 Cerumen removal	$\$2^{41}$ 87070 Throat culture
$0 99000 Specimen handling	$\$4^{05}$ 90471 Immunization admin
.71 81002 Urinalysis	$\$15^{20}$ 11200 Skin tag removal

ICD-9 Codes

____ 789.00 Abdominal pain	____ V70.0 Routine visit
____ 477.9 Allergies	____ 784.0 Headache
____ 285.9 Anemia	____ 401.1 Hypertension
____ 427.9 Arrhythmia	____ 458.9 Hypotension
____ 466.0 Bronchitis, acute	____ 272.4 Hyperlipidemia
____ 436 Cardiovascular accident	____ 410.91 Myocardial infarction
____ 414.00 Coronary artery disease	____ 382.90 Otitis media
____ 250.00 DM-controlled	____ 462 Pharyngitis
____ 782.3 Edema	____ 482 Pneumonitis
____ 780.79 Fatigue	____ 461.9 Sinusitis
____ 530.81 GERD	____ 599.0 Urinary tract infection

Name ____________________ Date __________

Prim ins ____________________ Sec ins ____________________

Self-pay __________ Co-pay __________ Pd-ck __________ CHG __________ Cash __________

Figure 4-1. Sample Medicare list of co-insurance due

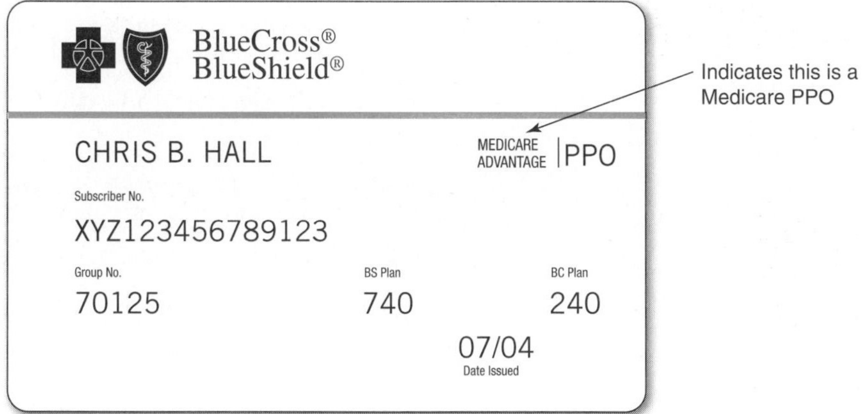

Figure 4-2. Sample managed care health insurance card

Regardless of whether or not the patient pays the co-payment prior to being seen, it is imperative that a member of the front desk staff collects the co-payment amount before the patient leaves the office. There is no valid excuse for patients with managed care insurance plans *not* to have their co-payment amount ready to pay. These patients are fully aware of the amount expected to be paid at the time of service because the co-pay is listed on the health insurance card. See Figure 4-2.

Medical offices have been known to reschedule patient's appointments for failure to pay the co-payment amount prior to being seen. This policy should be reflected in the practice's financial policy.

THE UNINSURED PATIENT

Uninsured patients should pay for services rendered at the time of the visit. If the uninsured patient was properly informed over the telephone when scheduling the appointment that payment is expected at the time of service (part of the Financial Policy), then the front-desk staff should not have a problem collecting payment from this patient on the day of the scheduled visit.

When the uninsured patient signs in at the front desk, the patient should be reminded that services are required to be paid in full *today*. If patients claim they do not have the funds to pay *today* and are not in immediate need of care, the front desk staff member should kindly explain that the appointment would need to be rescheduled. Adhering to this policy is another way of reducing future collections.

FORMS OF PAYMENT

Although cash and checks have always been a welcomed form of payment in the medical office, the ability to accept credit cards is a growing trend in many offices.

Payment by credit/debit is more convenient for many patients. With increased technology over the past decade, including online banking, consumers who engage in this form of banking use less paper checks than the 'computer-challenged' person.

Post-dated Checks

If a patient cannot pay a balance in full, and it is acceptable with the office manager, another means of payment may be a **post-dated check**, a check dated for the future.

For example, if the patient has a $300.00 balance, consider the following: Ask the patient to come to the office with three undated checks for $100.00 each. When the patient arrives, have the patient date one check for that day and the other checks for 30 and 60 days later, respectively.

Make sure the post-dated checks are kept in a separate, secure place apart from checks collected on a daily basis. This will prevent depositing the post-dated checks in advance. Depositing the post-dated checks in advance may cause them to bounce. This may wreak havoc with the patient's checking account, thus angering the patient. If this were to happen, the patient would surely call the office to complain that the office did not stick to their end of the deal, an example of poor customer service.

Payment Arrangements

When a patient has a very large balance, it is common for the patient to request a **payment arrangement**; a mutually agreed upon dollar amount to be paid (usually monthly) until the balance is paid in full.

The medical office should send the patient a contract to be signed by the patient detailing the arrangement. It should also be noted that failure to adhere to the contract might result in the patient's account being sent to collections (if this is the policy of the medical office). See Figure 4-3.

PATIENT STATEMENTS

Patient statements may be sent to patients for the following reasons:

- There is a balance due from patient after the insurance company has paid its portion
- As part of a monthly payment arrangement on a large balance

Payment Arrangement Agreement

ABC Medical Office
123 Anywhere Street
Anywhere, NJ 00001
(732) 555-5555

This payment arrangement is between the above-named provider and (insert patient's name), residing at (insert patient's address). The patient has agreed to pay provider the sum of (insert dollar amount) per month, due on the (insert date) of each month until the balance of (insert dollar amount) is paid in full.

Failure to adhere to the agreed terms may result in the patient's account being sent to an outside collection agency.

I, ______________________, understand and agree to the above terms.

Patient signature ____ **Date** __________

Provider's office representative signature ______________________ **Date** __________

Figure 4-3. Sample payment arrangement contract

David Operatomy, MD
123 Shady Lane
Anycity, USA 12345

ADDRESS SERVICE REQUESTED

ANY QUESTIONS PLEASE CALL 999- 999-9999
TAX ID: 123456789
PATIENT: PATIENT, JOHN Q

JOHN Q. PATIENT
202 MAIN STREET
ANYTOWN, USA 12345-0000

HEALTHCARE, USA
1234 MAIN STREET
ANYTOWN, USA 12345-0000

110485745000001000000000000000000901231199500000089003 235352*OW5QA0000000000

☐ Please check box if your address is incorrect or insurance information has changed, please indicate change(s) on reverse side.

STATEMENT

PLEASE DETACH AND RETUN TOP PORTION WITH YOUR PAYMENT

DATE	PATIENT	CPT	DESCRIPTION OF SERVICE	CHARGE	RECEIPT	ADJUSTMENT	LINE ITEM BALANCE
00/00/00	STEVE	99212	EST. PATIENT LEVEL 2	50.00	0.00	0.00	50.00
00/00/00	STEVE	99213	EST. PATIENT LEVEL 3	75.00	0.00	0.00	75.00
00/00/00	STEVE	99211	EST. PATIENT LEVEL 1	40.00	0.00	0.00	40.00

ACCOUNT NO.	CURRENT	30 DAYS	60 DAYS	90 DAYS	120 DAYS	TOTAL ACCOUNT BALANCE
031284 82	165.00	0.00	0.00	0.00	0.00	$165.00

PLEASE PAY THIS AMOUNT ♦♦♦♦ $165.00

Figure 4-4. Sample patient statement

- If the amount of the health insurance claim was applied to the patient's deductible
- A valid denial from the insurance company stating the bill is the patient's responsibility

Although most offices send patient statements on a monthly basis, techniques differ. Some offices send out patient statements with no return envelope, some will include a return envelope, and some will go a step further by affixing a stamp on the return envelope.

Many offices attach neon collection labels to their patient statements. These labels are used to grab the patient's attention with hope of prompt payment.

Regardless of the techniques used, it is crucial to be consistent in sending out patient statements. Imagine this scenario: A patient had an office visit on January 5. The insurance company paid its portion on February 15. The patient receives a bill from the office dated December 30.

It is unprofessional when patient statements are first sent months after the insurance company has paid. It makes the office staff look bad, as if they are not performing their job properly; another example of poor customer service.

Inconsistency with mailing out patient statements cannot only anger patients, but anger upper management as well. Remember, money due from patients is one of two components of the office's accounts receivable. See Figure 4-4.

CALLING THE PATIENT

In-office collections include making telephone calls to patients on outstanding bills. The goal of this telephone call is to collect money due the medical office. Good customer service is an important factor when making these calls. Some patients may need to 'vent' for different reasons; others may need an 'ear' to listen.

Being kind during the collection call can go a long way. This can be especially true when calling elderly patients. Remember the following when making collection calls:

- Offer the use of a credit/debit card for payment
- Suggest the patient pay with post-dated checks
- Suggest a payment arrangement

ROLE PLAYING ACTIVITY

Student A will play the role of the patient. Student B will play the role of the front desk receptionist.

Scenario: Ms. Smith, an established patient, has a managed care health insurance plan with a co-pay of $15.00 for office visits. She does not have money to pay up front today. Upon signing in, the following dialogue takes place:

Student B: "Good morning, Ms. Smith, how are you today? Your co-payment today is $15.00."

Student A: "Oh, I left my checkbook home. I'm sorry, can you bill me for that?"

Student B: "We do accept cash and credit cards also, Ms. Smith, which would you prefer?"

Student A: "Well, I have no cash on me, and my credit card is maxed to the limit. If you send me a bill, I promise to send in a check right away."

Student B: "I am sorry, Ms. Smith, although I wish I could do that for you, it is our policy to collect co-pays at the time of service."

Student A: "Oh, come on, I waited a week for this appointment, can I bring a check over tomorrow?"

Student B: "Unfortunately, Ms. Smith, if I did this for you, I would have to allow this for every patient who forgot their co-pay and I would be putting my job in jeopardy. We attempt to avoid this situation by the numerous signs we have posted in our office regarding co-payments and we also list this in our financial policy, which you singed at your first visit. Let me see when we can reschedule you to come in. Is Friday at 10:00 a.m. convenient for you?"

Student A: "Yes, I suppose that is O.K."

Student B: "Thank you for understanding, Ms. Smith, and we will see you Friday at 10:00 a.m."

STOP AND ANALYZE

The patient is probably not happy about having to reschedule her appointment; however, she will also probably never forget her co-payment again. While Ms. Smith tried to persuade the front desk receptionist to agree to a future payment, she was unsuccessful. The front desk receptionist was correct in adhering to the practice's financial policy.

This scenario is not uncommon in medical offices. It is imperative that medical office personnel not be swayed to break office policy rules, even for the most persisting patient.

ROLE PLAYING ACTIVITY

Student A will play the role of the medical office collections clerk. Student B will play the patient.

Scenario: Mrs. Feldman, an established patient, has a $150.00 balance for her January 10 office visit, $150.00 of which was applied to her deductible. The collections clerk must call Mrs. Feldman in an attempt to collect money, as there has been no payment from the patient, despite two patient statement mailings.

Student B: "Hello."

Student A: "Hi, Mrs. Feldman, this is ________________ calling from Dr. Field's office in reference to your outstanding balance of $150.00."

Student B: "Oh, yes, I got the bill. What is the bill for again?"

Student A: "The $150.00 balance is for your January 10 office visit, which was applied to your deductible. You should have received an Explanation of Benefits from your insurance company."

Student B: "Oh, I probably did, I have just been so busy lately."

Student A: "I can understand that. How would you like to take care of this *today*, Mrs. Feldman? For your convenience, we do accept credit cards."

Student B: "Oh, I cannot pay this in full today! Can I make payments on this?"

Student A: "Absolutely, Mrs. Feldman! We can set up a payment arrangement for you for $50.00 per month. How does that sound?"

Student B: "Well, that is a little high. Can we do $10.00 per month?"

Student A: "We might be able to do that, Mrs. Feldman, the only problem is we cannot see you in the office until the balance is paid in full, and at $10.00 per month, it would take 15 months before your account is paid in full."

STOP AND ANALYZE

If Mrs. Feldman is a regularly seen patient and is happy with the service she receives at the office, she is not going to want to wait 15 months before she is seen again.

Let us assume that she is happy with the physician's service:

ROLE PLAYING ACTIVITY

Student B: "Oh, I can't wait that long to see the doctor! O.K., I suppose I can pay $50.00 per month."

Student A: "Great! Let's set this up. Which day of the month is best for you as a due date?"

Student B: "The 30th of the month would be best for me."

Student A: "Great, Mrs. Feldman. I will make a notation in the computer that you agree to monthly payments of $50.00 per month, due on the 30th of each month. Today is the 7th, so your first payment will be due the 30th of this month. I will send you two copies of our payment arrangement agreement. Please keep one for your records, sign the second copy and send it back to our office with your first payment."

Student B: "Great, I will do that."

Student A: "Mrs. Feldman, one more thing. I have to inform you that failure to adhere to the agreement could result in your account being turned over to collections, so try not to miss a payment."

Student B: "I understand, thank you."

STOP AND ANALYZE

This scenario was a win-win situation because:

- The patient agreed to a payment arrangement.
- The collections clerk was able to convince the patient to agree to $50.00 per month instead of $10.00 per month; therefore, collecting *more* money in a *faster* time frame.
- The collections clerk demonstrated a professional attitude and fine customer service skills throughout the telephone conversation, both important factors in sustaining patient relationships.

CHAPTER SUMMARY

- Verifying health insurance coverage prior to the patient's appointment is an aid in determining the patient's responsibility for payment.
- Reimbursement is made at 80% of the allowed amount of the payer's fee schedule for indemnity/traditional health insurance plans.
- Medicare is a government plan in which reimbursement for most services is made at 80%.
- Co-insurance is associated with indemnity, traditional, and Medicare health insurance plans.
- Co-payments are associated with managed care plans.
- Supplemental plans are those intended to cover the cost of deductibles and/or co-insurance.
- Payment policies should be reflected in the practice's financial policy.
- Collecting co-insurance, co-payments, and money due from uninsured patients up-front are ways of reducing in-office collections.
- Post-dated checks and payment arrangements are methods of payment for those patients unable to pay their balance in full.
- Consistency in the mailing of patient statements aids in maintaining the office's accounts receivable and is also an example of good customer service.
- Good customer service is an important factor when calling the patient.

REVIEW QUESTIONS

Multiple choice: Pick the best answer to each question.

1. The dollar amount an insurance company deems fair for a specific service or procedure is called the ________________.
   A. assigned fee
   B. allowed amount
   C. scheduled amount
   D. co-insurance

2. A payer's list of allowed amounts for all services and procedures is called a ________________.
   A. payer list
   B. payable schedule
   C. fee schedule
   D. CPT list

3. A bill reflecting the patient's responsibility is called a/an ________________.
   A. explanation of benefits
   B. health insurance claim
   C. fee schedule
   D. patient statement

4. A government plan in which reimbursement for most services and procedures is paid at 80% of the allowed amount is called ________________.
   A. Medicare
   B. Medigap
   C. Managed Care
   D. none of the above

5. A form listing CPT, HCPCS, and ICD-9-CM codes used to record services and diagnoses is called a/an ________________.
   A. fee schedule
   B. superbill
   C. explanation of benefits
   D. health insurance claim

Fill in the blank: Complete each statement in the space provided.

6. A type of insurance plan in which reimbursement is made at 80% of the allowed amount is known as a/an ________________________________ plan or a/an ________________________________ plan.

7. A secondary insurance plan intended to cover the cost of the patient's deductible and/or 20% co-insurance is called a/an ________________________________ plan.

8. Patients with no health insurance are called ______________________________.

9. A check dated for the future is called a/an ______________________________.

10. A mutually agreed upon dollar amount to be paid until the balance is paid in full is called a/an ______________________________.

Short answer: Answer each question with a short statement.

11. List four reasons for sending out patient statements.

____

____

____

____

12. If a patient's co-insurance amount due is known at the time of service, what are the benefits of collecting this amount up front?

____

____

____

____

13. What is the importance of keeping post-dated checks separate from checks collected on a daily basis?

____

____

____

____

14. Why is consistency important in sending out patient statements?

____

____

____

____

15. What form of payment is a growing trend in many offices and what is the benefit to the patient?

16. What is an important factor to remember when making telephone calls to patients and why is this important?

17. List various ways of reducing in-office collections and maintaining the office's accounts receivable.

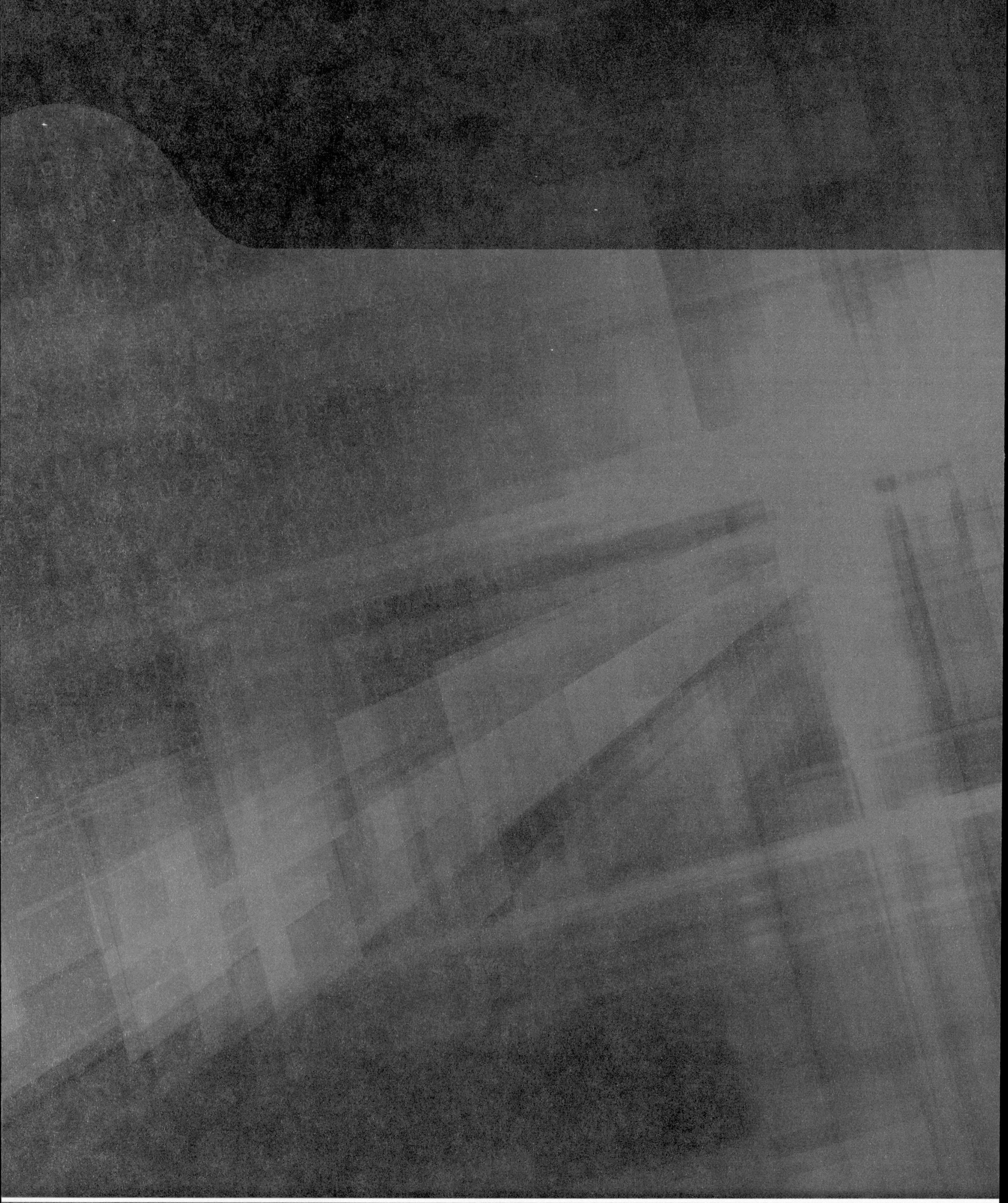

Chapter 5

The Appeal Process

OBJECTIVES

Upon completion of this chapter, the student should be able to:

- List reasons for health insurance claim denial.
- Understand steps in the appeal process.
- Explain necessary documentation needed for the appeal.
- Define key terms.

KEY TERMS

Denied

Explanation of Benefits (EOB)

Non-covered benefit

Unauthorized

THE DENIED CLAIM

Submission of a health insurance claim to a payer does not guarantee payment to the provider. Frequently, claims are denied (refused to grant payment for), resulting in delayed reimbursement for the provider. Reasons for denials can include, but are not limited to:

- Insurance coverage not yet effective
- Insurance coverage terminated prior to the date of service
- Insured's name does not match the payer's database
- Incorrect health insurance identification number
- Other primary insurance on file
- Diagnosis code does not meet requirements for procedure or service
- Procedure or service is considered a non-covered benefit (not a covered benefit in a payer's master benefit list)
- Procedure or service is unauthorized (authorization or approval not obtained prior to treatment)
- Invalid CPT, ICD-9-CM, or HCPCS level 2 codes
- Maximum benefits reached for this procedure or service
- Submission of claim exceeds payer's claim filing deadline

These reasons for denial are listed on the Explanation of Benefits (EOB) form sent by the payer to the physician (or patient) detailing claim benefits. See Figure 5-1.

THE APPEAL PROCESS: RESPONDING TO THE DENIED CLAIM

Deciphering the EOB for denial explanation does not always result in the appeal of the claim. Frequently, a claim is denied through no fault of the medical office. If either the medical office or the patient feels the claim was denied in error or that reimbursement should have been made, one or both parties may call the insurance company to inform them of the error or provide them with the necessary information to reprocess the claim for reimbursement. Table 5-1 lists reasons and suggested actions for the denied claim.

STOP AND ANALYZE

Have you ever had a claim denied for medical service? How did you handle the situation? What was the outcome?

Provider Name
Provider Address

Winston Wagner, DO
00330 Spring Lake Rd
Spring Lake, NJ 00004
NPI# 0000260000

Policyholder: Vera Vonable
Patient: Victor Vonable
Patient #: Vonvi 000
ID #/Group #: 339ZQ4372/996644
Claim #: 26-QRZ549
Date: 02-27-YY

Employee Name & Address
Vera Vonable
0030 Oakhurst Rd
Oakhurst, NJ 00007

Customer Service Information
(800) 555-5555

Date of Service	Procedure	Total Amount	Not Covered	Reason Code	Allowed Amount	Deductible Amount	Co-pay/ Co-ins Amount	Paid At	Payment Amount
02-01-YY	99203	$100.00	$100.00	02					$0.00
Totals		$100.00	$100.00						$0.00
								Other Insurance Credits or Adjustments	
								Total Net Payment	$0.00
								Total Patient Responsibility	$100.00

Accumulators
Your $250 deductible has been satisfied.

Payment to: Check No. Amount
$0.00

Service Code
Office visit

Reason Code Description
02- Coverage terminated prior to date of service

Messages:

Figure 5-1. Sample EOB form for a denied claim

Table 5-1. Reasons and suggested actions for denied claims

Denial Reason	Suggested Action
Insurance coverage not yet effective	Patient should contact the physician's office with correct insurance information.
Insurance coverage terminated	Patient should contact the physician's office with correct insurance information.
Other primary insurance on file	Patient should contact the physician's office with correct insurance information.
Insured's name does not match payer's database	Biller should check copy of ID card to see if incorrect name was a result of a typographical error.
Incorrect health insurance identification number	Biller should check copy of ID card to see if incorrect number was a result of a typographical error.
Diagnosis code does not meet requirements for procedure of service	If not a billing error, file an appeal with the insurance company.
Procedure or service is considered a non-covered benefit	An appeal may be attempted. If appeal is denied, the balance is the patient's responsibility.
Procedure or service is unauthorized	If the physician's office had the responsibility to obtain authorization, the physician decides whether to write off the claim balance. If the responsibility to obtain authorization was the patient's, the patient is responsible for paying the claim balance.
Maximum benefits reached for this service	Attempt an appeal. If denied, responsibility for paying the claim balance is the patient's.
Submission of claim exceeds payer's filing deadline	Biller may attempt an appeal with explanation for late filing. If denied, the physician must approve a write-off of the claim balance.
Subscriber did not follow guidelines regarding emergency room visits	Patient may attempt appeal explaining why guidelines were not followed.

APPEALS DOCUMENTATION

Some payers have a specific form for filing a claim inquiry or appeal requests; one such payer is Medicare. See Figure 5-2.

Notice that Medicare offers the following five levels in the Part A (hospital coverage) and Part B (medical coverage) appeals process:

- Redetermination
- Reconsideration
- Administrative Law Judge (ALJ) Hearing
- Departmental Appeal Board Review
- Judicial Review in U.S. District Court

When appealing a claim, it is important to remember the following:

- Write down the date, the name of the person contacted, and details of all telephone conversations and/or correspondence relating to the denied claim in question
- Keep original documents in the physician's office and send photocopies to the insurance company, with a letter outlining why the claim should be covered
- Include copies of the patient's records (progress notes, lab results, diagnostic testing results) to assist when appealing for reasons of medical necessity
- Adhere to the payer's appeal filing deadlines
- Request a written reply

See Figures 5-3 through 5-5 for samples of appeal letters.

MEDICARE PART B CLAIM INQUIRY/APPEAL REQUEST FORM

Fields marked with an * are REQUIRED for an Appeal Request

This form may be used for one or more claims concerning the same issue. If your request involves multiple claims, you may attach a copy of your Standard Paper Remittance (SPR) to this form and highlight the services you want reviewed.

Please mail this form and pertinent documentation (Certificate of Medical Necessity, operative notes, test results, etc.) to:

New Jersey Providers Mail to:
Empire Medicare Services
P.O. Box 69202
Harrisburg, PA 17106-9202

New York Providers Mail to:
Empire Medicare Services
P.O. Box 2280
Peekskill, NY 10566-2280

Date of Request: / /

CLAIM INFORMATION

PROVIDER NUMBER:	***PATIENT HEALTH INSURANCE CLAIM NUMBER (HIC):**
***PROVIDER NAME & ADDRESS:**	***PATIENT NAME & ADDRESS:**
***INTERNAL CONTROL NUMBER(S):**	***PROCEDURE CODE(S):**
***DATES OF SERVICE:**	**BILLED AMOUNT:**

***SPR DATE:** / /

***REQUEST FOR: APPEAL: ☐ INQUIRY: ☐**
The date of the Standard Paper Remittance (SPR) for the claim in question:
If the appeal concerns Medicare Secondary Payment, please indicate if you participate with the Primary insurance company _____ participate _____do not participate

***REASON FOR APPEAL/INQUIRY (AND LATE FILING EXPLANATION IF APPLICABLE):**

____

____

____

____

____

* **If your request has exceeded the time limit for an appeal, please include the reason for late filing with your request.**
* **If requesting an appeal of an unassigned claim, as the patient's representative, complete the Appointment of Representative Form (CMS 1696-U4). Otherwise, requests on behalf of the patient can be made through this form or any written statement; however, the outcome of the appeal will only be disclosed to the patient.**

***REQUESTER'S NAME & TITLE:**	**TELEPHONE NUMBER:**
***REQUESTER'S SIGNATURE:**	**DATE SIGNED:**

SMC3123 Rev. 01/11/2005

Figure 5-2. Sample Medicare Part B claim inquiry/appeal request form *Courtesy of The Centers for Medicare and Medicaid Services http://www.cms.hhs.gov.*

Insurance Company
Address

Date

Dear Mr. ___________:

We have received the explanation of benefits for the patient, Mr. Robert Crawford. However, we believe the charges, totaling **$480.00** for February 25, 20XX through March 14, 20XX, have been considered incorrectly.

The EOB states that the March 15th charge of **$80.00** is not a medical necessity. When I spoke to you at the claims center earlier this week, your explanation of the denial was because the patient is not homebound; the insurance company believes the visit was for patient convenience and not medically necessary.

In reviewing the nurse's notes for each skilled nursing visit medical necessity appears to have been established. The March 15th visit should not have been denied. A new infusion therapy was started on that date and the patient required instruction on drug administration.

Skilled nursing visits are a medical necessity to follow up on how well the patient is learning; in this instance, errors in the patient's technique were in fact discovered. Throughout the therapy the patient was fatigued, weak, and felt sick. The patient also felt overwhelmed with the therapies, requiring further instruction and reinforcement. The results of not having skilled nursing visits could lead to further complications, such as the patient not following the drug schedule or performing inaccurate drug administration.

It appears that a review of the nurse's notes would support the medical necessity of the nursing charges. Please reconsider the denied portion of the charges and issue a payment to Valu Home Care in the amount of **$80.00**.

Sincerely,

____

Collections Manager, Valu Home Care

Figure 5-3. Sample appeal letter for "not medically necessary" denial of charges

Insurance Company
Address

Date

Dear Ms. ___________,

I am writing to you in regards to a claim submitted by White Oaks Hospital for my daughter, [name]. The charges were rendered on August 30, 20XX, and totaled $23,716.91. ABC Insurance Company has considered the charges and made a payment of $18,269,86, but this was after a penalty of $1,500.00 was deducted from the payment.

My daughter was involved in a serious car accident. We were unaware of a required preauthorization procedure and, under the circumstances, didn't think to investigate the policy booklet about preauthorizing inpatient hospital stays. The policy booklet does state that the preauthorization hotline must be called within three days of the patient's admittance to the hospital for emergency situations. However, both the hospital and attending physician were preferred providers. I called the PPO agency and they advised me that it \s the medical provider's responsibility, if they are preferred providers, to initiate the preauthorization. [Name] from [name] PPO network, at (800) 555-1234, extension 567, was my contact for this information. Because of this, I believe the benefit penalty was applied in error.

Please reconsider the charges and issue the additional payment to the hospital. Thank you,

Sincerely,

[insured's name]

Figure 5-4. Sample appeal letter concerning reduction of payment for failure to preauthorize treatment

Insurance Company
Address

Date

Dear Claims Review Department:

I am writing to you in regards to a claim submitted by Home Health Agency [medical provider] for [patient]. The charges were rendered on [date] and totaled [claim dollar total]. [Health plan] has denied payment for this procedure, stating that the home health agency was not licensed.

The State of Kentucky does not require a home health agency to be a licensed provider. The current condition requires that the services of a home health agency be obtained. Home health agency visits are a covered expense under my plan. I am requesting that you reconsider your denial of the claim for this service and immediately authorize payment. I am including, with this appeal letter, documentation that supports this statement.

As a member of [health plan], I am requesting your reconsideration of this denial and that you extend the coverage for me. If there is any additional information I could provide to you that would expedite this matter, please feel free to contact me. Thank you for your time and assistance in this matter.

Sincerely,

[insured's name]

Enclosures:

____

____

Figure 5-5. Sample appeal letter for "place of service" denial

CHAPTER SUMMARY

- Health insurance claims submission does not guarantee payment of a claim.
- Explanations for a denied claim are listed on the EOB sent from the payer.
- Either the medical office or the patient may request an appeal of a denied claim.
- It is important to include all necessary patient information (for example: progress notes and medical records) and to adhere to the payer's guidelines when filing an appeal.

REVIEW QUESTIONS

Fill in the blank: Complete each statement in the space provided.

1. A form detailing claim benefits is known as the ______________________________.

Short answer: Answer each question with a short statement.

2. List five reasons for claim denial.

____

____

____

____

____

3. What is the suggested action when a claim is denied for other primary insurance on file?

____

____

____

____

____

4. What might a physician decide to do if an appeal request is denied for a claim submitted that "exceeded the payer's filing deadline"?

____

____

____

____

____

5. What are the five levels in the Medicare appeal process?

6. What are five important details to remember when appealing a claim?

Define the following key terms.

7. Denied

8. Explanation of Benefits

9. Non-covered benefit

10 Unauthorized

Long answer: Use the information presented to complete the task.

11. Consider the following scenario and write a sample appeal letter, as the insured, to the insurance company requesting reconsideration of reimbursement for the claim.

Fact: Mary and Steve Jones were visiting family out of state during the winter holiday. During the visit, their 4-year-old daughter awoke in the middle of the night with severe ear pain. Saturday at 2 a.m., Mary and Steve took their daughter to the emergency room at a local hospital. The emergency room doctor confirmed that their child had an ear infection; the fluid in her ear was not draining properly because a tube (placed in her ear six months earlier) was becoming dislodged.

EOB: The claim was denied because the insured did not notify the insurance company of the emergency room visit within 48 hours.

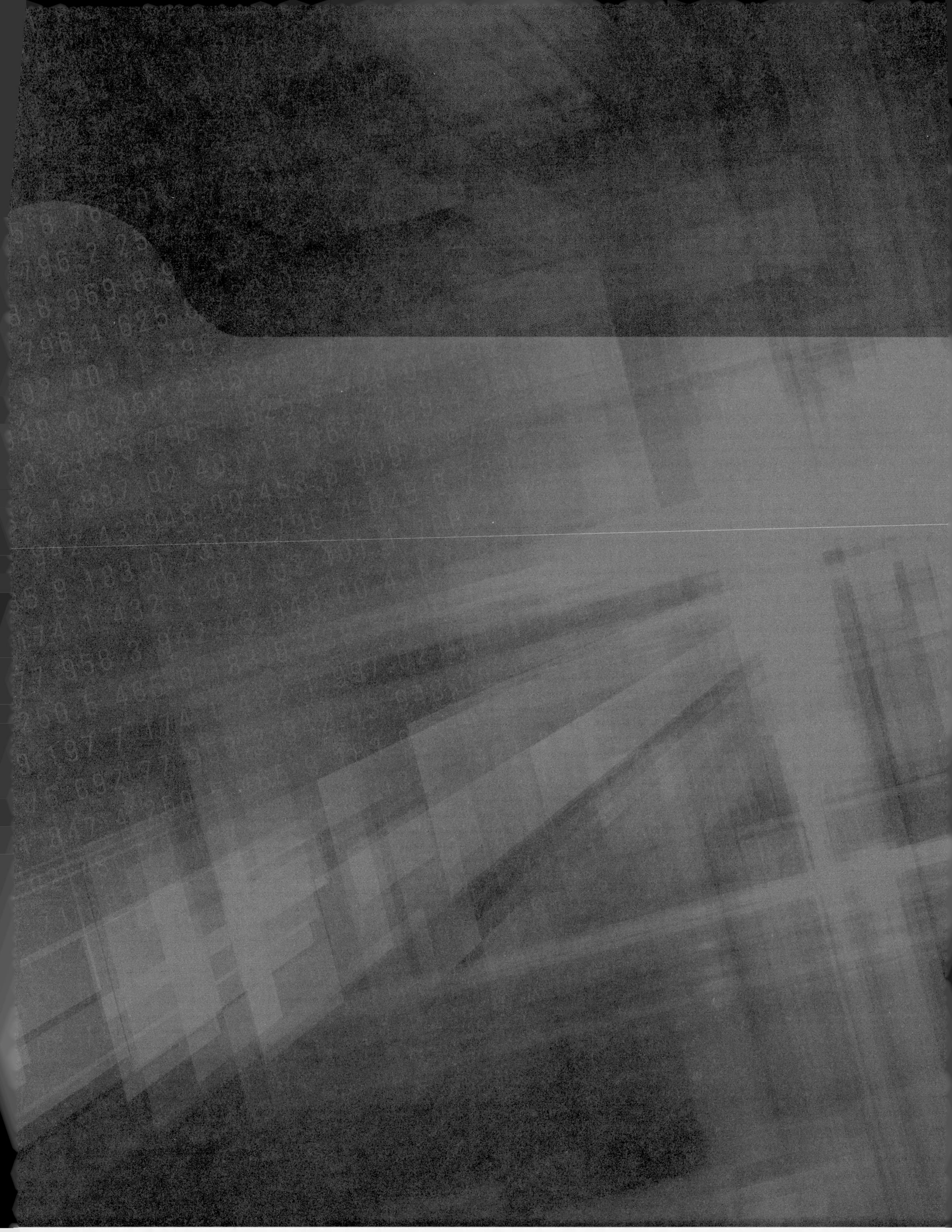

Chapter 6

Additional Income for the Medical Office

OBJECTIVES

Upon completion of this chapter, the student should be able to:

- Understand laws regarding charging fees for medical record requests.
- Explain the additional resources of income for the medical office.
- Discuss the rationale behind charging fees for form completion.
- Define key terms.

KEY TERMS

Administrative

Centers for Medicare and Medicaid Services (CMS)

Clinical

Current Procedural Terminology (CPT)

Deposition

Medical expert witness

Narrative report

SUPPLEMENTAL SOURCES OF INCOME

Apart from collecting for clinical services, those which involve direct observation and treatment of living patients, medical offices may charge and collect fees for specific administrative duties; those pertaining to administration (group of people who manage; for example: front office duties involving paperwork).

A physician's office may request patients, businesses, or attorney's to pay for the following administrative services:

- Medical records copying
- Form completion
- Narrative report (a report that provides information to insurance carriers, other healthcare professionals, attorneys, and the court system)
- Missed appointments
- Medical expert witness

Medical Records Copying

Under HIPAA, a covered entity can only charge "reasonable" cost-based fees for providing copies of medical records to patients. The fee for this charge should be listed in either the medical office's financial policy statement, or posted conspicuously at the front desk. See Figure 6-1. Some states provide the first copy of the medical record for free. See Appendix II for a list of fees by state.

Form Completion

There are no federal or state guidelines for what providers may charge to fill out forms, such as those required by payers, businesses, schools, government, or other entities.

Although there is a Current Procedural Terminology (CPT) code, which is assigned for services and procedures (code 99080 – special reports, such as

Attention Patients:

The fee for copying your medical records is $1.00 per page; please allow us 14 days to complete your request.

Thank you,

Doctor X and staff

Figure 6-1. Sample sign for medical records copying fee

insurance forms, more than the information conveyed in the usual medical communications or standard reporting form), this code is not reimbursable by most payers. Therefore, providers throughout the United States may opt to charge the requesting party of the time involved in providing this type of service. These forms might be related to the following:

- Social Security disability or Social Security income benefits
- School exam/immunization schedule
- Sports exam
- Pre-employment exam
- Temporary disability benefits

STOP AND ANALYZE

Do you think it is fair for physicians to charge a fee for form completion? Why or why not?

Narrative Report

When an attorney or other entity requests a narrative report from a physician, the requesting party must obtain authorization for "Release of Information" signed by the patient or the patient's guardian. See Figure 6-2.

A thorough narrative report should contain:

- Report date
- Patient name and age
- Date of treatment or services
- Patient chief complaint
- Medical/dental history
- Other treatments for the disorder
- Description of accident, incident, or illness, including cause
- Objective clinical findings
- Diagnosis
- Treatment
- Prognosis

See Figure 6-3.

Missed Appointment Fee

Medical offices may legally charge the patient a fee for a missed appointment. This fee is not a charge for service itself, but rather is a charge for a missed business opportunity. The fee for a missed appointment must be listed in the medical office's financial policy statement.

Name or specific identification of the person(s), or class of persons, authorized to make the requested disclosure:

TO:	**Patient Name:** **Address:** **Date of Birth:** **Social Security Number:**

I authorize the disclosure of all protected medical information for the purpose of review and evaluation in connection with a legal claim. I expressly request that all covered entities under HIPPA identified above disclose any and all full and complete protected medical information, including the following:

- All medical records, including inpatient, outpatient and emergency room treatment, all clinical charts, progress notes, reports, documents, correspondence, test results, statements, questionnaires/histories, office and doctor's handwritten notes, and records received by other physicians.
- All autopsy, laboratory, histology, cytology, pathology, radiology, CT Scan, MRI, echocardiogram and cardiac catheterization reports.
- All radiology films, mammograms, myelograms, CT scans, photographs, bone scans, pathology, cytology, histology, autopsy, irnmunohistochemistry specimens, cardiac catheterization videos, CDs, films, reels, and echocardiogram videos. I expressly authorize and request the release of any original X-ray films.
- All pharmacy/prescription records including NDC numbers and drug information handouts/monographs.
- All billing records including all statements, itemized bills, and insurance records.
- All incident reports, accident reports, witness statements, or similar records.

This authorization does apply to psychotherapy notes, psychiatric or psychological records.
I understand that the information in my health record may include information pertaining to the treatment of drug and alcohol abuse, acquired immunodeficiency syndrome (AIDS), or human immunodeficiency virus (HIV), sexually transmitted diseases, tuberculosis or genetics.
THIS INFORMATION WILL ALSO BE RELEASED UNLESS YOU INITIAL HERE:
DO NOT RELEASE ________.

This information may be disclosed to and used by the following individual or organization:

Name: ____

Address: ____

For the purpose of: ____

I understand that authorizing the disclosure of this health information is voluntary. I can refuse to sign this authorization.
I acknowledge the right to revoke this authorization, in writing, by sending written notification to you at the above referenced address. However, I understand that any actions already taken in reliance on this authorization cannot be reversed, and my revocation will not affect those actions.
I acknowledge the potential for information disclosed pursuant to this authorization to be subject to redisclosure by the recipient and to no longer be protected under 45 CFR 164.508. This information may be exchanged among counsel, expert consultants, insurance representatives or others involved in litigation of my personal injury action.
I understand that the covered entity to whom this authorization is directed may not condition treatment, payment, enrollment or eligibility benefits on whether or not I sign the authorizations.
Any facsimile, copy or photocopy of the authorization shall authorize you to release the records herein.
This authorization shall be in force and effect until the claim has been concluded, at which time this authorization expires.

Signature of Patient or Legal Representative	Dated
If signed by Legal Representative, Relationship to Patient (signature of witness required)	Signature of Witness

Figure 6-2. Sample Authorization to Release Form

Smith Rehabilitation Consultants
P.O. Box 999, Carbondale, IL 61111
Providing Services in these Locations:
Chicago, Bloomington, Urbana, Danville, Decatur, Clinton, Galesburg, Belleville, Canton, Kewanee, Monmouth, Fairbury, Macomb
Phone (309) 444-5555 Fax (309) 444-5555

Independent Functional Evaluation Post-Offer Testing & Job Analysis
Software Products & Testing Devices Case Review & Litigation Support

---

May 2, 20XX

Emilio Gomez, MD
Central Illinois Orthopeadics
1015 South Main
Trenton, IL 61111

RE: Bob Vandermay / FCE Report

Dear Dr. Gomez:

On your prescription, a functional capacity evaluation was performed on the above-named client on April 26, 20XX. The results of the evaluation are contained in the attached report. If you have any questions regarding this report, please contact me. Thank you for your referral of Bob Vandermay for evaluation.

Sincerely,

Darrell Schapmire, MS

cc: Candace Wells—Global Insurance

Figure 6-3. Sample Narrative Report (*continues*)

Functional Capacity Evaluation

Smith Rehabilitation Consultants

Client Name: Bob Vandermay
Date of Service: 04-26-XX
Date of Injury: 10-29-XX
Employer: Wiley Group
Carrier: Global Insurance
Diagnosis: A/P L5-S1 Fusion with ORIF, Ventral Hernia Repair with Mesh

Case Number: 10720778
Physician: Emilio Gomez, MD
Date of Surgery: 11-29-XX
Job Title: Construction Inspector
Rehab Vendor: NA

Bob Vandermay was referred to Smith Rehabilitation Consultants for a functional capacity evaluation. The purpose of the test was to determine the client's functional abilities and to make appropriate recommendations. Test results and recommendations are summarized in the first four sections of this report. More detailed information related to the data collection begin in Section 5. Smith Rehabilitation Consultants' test protocol is a "psychophysical" approach. Material handling activities are terminated when the client indicates that a maximum level of performance has been obtained or if the evaluator believes that the point of biomechanical breakdown has been reached. This protocol cross-references most data obtained during the test. **Material handling activities are cross-referenced on the testing devices. This equipment is patented and manufactured by Smith Rehabilitation Consultants. Upper extremity test results are cross-referenced with Simultaneous Bilateral Force Testing, a method that has been validated by research conducted at Millikin University, Decatur, Illinois. This research has been published in the July-September 2002 issue of the *Journal of Hand Therapy*.**

SECTION 1: TEST SYNOPSIS

AREA EVALUATED	RESULTS	FOUND IN
Client Effort	**Consistent**	**Sections 2, 3, 5, 6, 8, 9**
Client Motivation	**Good**	**Sections 2, 3, 5, 6, 8, 9**
Overt Pain Behaviors	**Absent**	**Sections 2, 3, 5, 6, 8, 9**
Symptom Magnification Questionnaires	**Negative**	**Section 6**
Abnormal Test Responses	**Absent**	**Sections 2 3, 5, 6, 8, 9**
Physical Demand Level of Client's Job	**Heavy (Estimated)**	**Section 7**
Physical Demand Level Demonstrated by Client	**Light-Medium**	**Section 8**
Primary Recommendations	**Assignment to Work at the Light Physical Demand Level**	**Section 4**

SECTION 2: SUMMARY AND OVERVIEW OF FINDINGS

The results of this test indicate an exceptionally consistent effort on the part of the client, Bob Vandermay. The pain questionnaires are negative for symptom magnification. Waddell Testing was negative in 4/5 categories of non-physical low back pain. There was an absence of overt pain behaviors during the clinical evaluation and the functional activities. No cogwheeling was noted during manual strength testing or during the lifting evaluation. A cursory evaluation of the client's hand strengths reveals normal and symmetrical strengths, as would be expected in the testing of these uninvolved parts of the body. Therefore, a complete hand strength assessment for the purpose of assessing validity of effort was not indicated. **The client's baseline lifting capacities of unmarked steel weights correlated with the corresponding lifts performed on the Lever Arm, indicating good consistency of effort.** Based upon the information gathered during this evaluation, valid recommendations can be made for this case.

Figure 6-3. Sample Narrative Report (*continued*)

Mr. Vandermay appears to be mechanically stable. Leg lengths are equal in the supine position. The ilial crests and ASIS are level when the client stands. There is equal excursion of the PSIS during lumbar flexion. Provocative testing fails to produce an asymmetry in the pelvic girdle. These findings indicate the client has apparent stability in the lumbar spine.

Dural stretch testing (supine position, non-painful straight leg raise followed by adduction of the leg past midline, internal rotation of the leg and dorsiflexion of the ankle) is negative bilaterally. The Slump Test (seated posture, followed by lumbar flexion and cervical flexion) is similarly negative. These findings indicate a likely absence of nerve root impingement in the lower lumbar spine.

Although ranges of motion are diminished in the lumbar spine, gross strengths throughout the body are within normal limits. All other ranges of motion are completely normal, as would be expected.

Unrelated to the accident which resulted in Mr. Vandermay's back injury is the fact that he has had a ventral hernia repair that required in the implantation of mesh. This is the client's second such surgery. The mesh used for the second procedure is approximately 24 square inches in size. Although not directly related to his accident, this factor, in conjunction with the client's lengthy history of back problems argues for caution when returning Mr. Vandermay to work.

Mr. Vandermay lifted 30-40 pounds on the day of this test, with the amount of weight lifted varying with the height from which the lifts are initiated. These results were validated by cross-referencing his performance on the Lever Arm, a device on which workloads cannot be accurately estimated by visual inspection. **According to recently-completed research, the odds of an individual being able to estimate five different workloads on this device with no more than 25% error for each estimation are less than 1 in 1,000. Since five different baseline lifts of unmarked steel weights were cross-referenced on the Lever Arm with a different configuration of barbell weights for each Lever Arm lift, these results should be considered as reflective of the client's best effort.** The recommendations (found in Section 4) are based on a thorough investigation of consistency of effort. It is not likely that Mr.

Vandermay could safely return to a workplace, provided his work falls within the physical parameters described in Section 4. Work outside of these parameters may put him at increased risk for re-injury.

SECTION 3: LEGITIMACY OF EFFORT

Mr. Vandermay passed the following validity criteria:

1. Six of seven pain questionnaires negative for symptom magnification.
2. Absence of overt pain behaviors during clinical evaluation and during functional testing.
3. Absence of cogwheeling during manual strength testing and during the lifting evaluation.
4. Waddell Testing negative in 4/5 categories.
5. Good correlation between baseline lifts of unmarked steel bars as compared to the corresponding lifts performed on the Lever Arm.

SECTION 4: RECOMMENDATIONS

1. Mr. Vandermay should be released for work that would be classified at the "light-medium" physical demand level, with work-related activities falling within these parameters:
   A. Occasional bilateral lifts initiated from grade level and terminated at the waist level not to exceed 10 pounds.
   B. Occasional bilateral lifts initiated at 10" above grade level and terminated at waist level not to exceed 30-35 pounds.
   C. Occasional bilateral lifts initiated at 20" above grade level and terminated at waist level not to exceed 35-40 pounds.
   D. Occasional bilateral lifts between waist and chest level not to exceed 30-35 lbs.

Figure 6-3. Sample Narrative Report (*continues*)

E. Occasional bilateral lifts between waist and eye level not to exceed 20 lbs.
F. Occasional unilateral lifts initiated at 10" above grade level and terminated at waist level not to exceed
30 pounds.
G. Occasional carrying of up to 40 pounds for distances less than 20 feet, provided the workload is lifted with the knuckles no closer than 20" above grade level.
H. No lifting above eye level.
I. No work above or below grade level.
J. No ambulation over uneven, unstable or slippery surfaces.
K. Work to the client's tolerance with regard to activities that require flexion, rotation or lateral flexion of the cervical spine.
L. Opportunity to stand, sit or otherwise change body position to maintain a reasonable level of comfort throughout the day.

2. Medical correlation for the above is required.

SECTION 5: BARRIERS TO REHABILITATION AND CASE RESOLUTION

1. Nature and extent of physical injuries.
2. Significant history of multiple, previous back injuries.

SECTION 6: SUBJECTIVE REPORTS AND BEHAVIORAL OBSERVATIONS

Symptom magnification, assessed with commonly-administered written instruments, produced the following results:

1. Quantified Pain Drawing, negative, with a score of 5.
2. Visual Analog Scale, negative, with a score of 2 centimeters.
3. Waddell Disability Questionnaire, negative, with a score of /9.
4. Inappropriate Symptoms Questionnaire, negative, with a score of 1/5.
5. 0-10+ Pain Rating Scale, negative, with a score of 3/10.
6. Modified Somatic Perceptions Scale, negative, with a score of 7.
7. Oswestry Low Back Inventory, positive, with a score of 50%.

The client rated his current level of disability at 70%. He rated his chances for having a good recovery at 0%.

On the Quantified Pain Drawing, Mr. Vandermay indicates centralized dull aching and stabbing pain that spreads from left to right at the waistline. The remaining instruments are unremarkable for pain and/or dysfunction in the performance of daily activities.

During the intake interview, Mr. Vandermay stated prolonged sitting, standing, bending at the waist (flexion as well as extension), overhead work (changing a light bulb), and percussive forces through the feet are activities or conditions that increase his pain. He reports that he is no longer able to golf, ride a motorcycle, camp or go boating. He lays down and relaxes to control the pain. The client states that he is unable to sleep on his stomach. He reports being awakened 4-5 times a night with back pain. The worst pain is at the waistline. He has left lower extremity pain that radiates to the knee from time to time. He states that he has bilateral hip pain in the joints when his symptoms peak. Mr. Vandermay is stiff and sore in the morning, but he tries to walk 2 miles a day. The left foot feels "cold and damp" much of the time. He changes body position to help control the symptoms.

Mr. Vandermay arises by 5:30 AM. During the day, he plays guitar and takes a walk. He has no special daily routine. No other details regarding his daily activity were provided. The client retires between 9:00 PM and midnight.

Figure 6-3. Sample Narrative Report (*continued*)

SECTION 7: JOB DESCRIPTION

No official job description has been received. The information in this section was obtained from the client during the intake interview. Mr. Vandermay was a "construction inspector" whose particular specialty was concrete inspection. Duties included performing Slump Tests and Air Entrapment Tests. Some supervisory duties were involved from time to time. The job required working outside throughout the construction season. Collectively, the duties involved frequent bending, squatting and kneeling (to perform the various tests). Ambulation could be on uneven, unstable or slippery surfaces. Some work above grade level was required. Lifting of weight up to 100 pounds is reported to be required on the job.

SECTION 8: PHYSICAL TESTING RESULTS

1. **Material Handling Assessment**: The client was tested for his ability to perform various material handling tasks. Unmarked steel weights were used in the "Baseline Testing." **The results were on the Lever Arm.**

Activity	Baseline Testing (Using Unmarked Steel Weights)	Cross-Reference Testing (Using Lever Arm)	Correlation Between Baselines and Performance?
Bilateral Floor to Waist Lift	**10.35 lbs.**	NA	NA
Bilateral 10" to Waist Lift	**32.85 lbs.**	37.01 lbs.	Yes (12.1% Increase)
Bilateral 15" to Waist Lift	**32.85 lbs.**	37.86 lbs.	Yes (15.2% Increase)
Bilateral 20" to Waist Lift	**40.35 lbs.**	43.67 lbs.	Yes (8.2% Increase)
Right Unilateral 10" Waist to Chest Lift	**29.10 lbs.**	27.45 lbs.	Yes (5.6% Decrease)
Left Unilateral 10" Waist to Chest Lift	**29.10 lbs.**	27.45 lbs.	Yes (5.6% Decrease)
Bilateral Waist to Chest Lift	**29.10 lbs.**	NA	NA
Bilateral Waist to Eye Lift	**20.00 lbs.**	NA	NA
Bilateral Waist to Overhead	**Not Tested, Contraindicated**	NA	NA
Bilateral Carry (Preceded by lift from 10")	**32.85 lbs. for 20 feet**	NA	NA
Right Unilateral Carry (Preceded by lift from 10")	**25.35 lbs. for 20 feet**	NA	NA
Left Unilateral Carry (Preceded by lift from 10")	**25.35 lbs. for 20 feet**	NA	NA

The biomechanical positioning and requirements of the Baseline and Cross-Reference lifts are nearly identical. Therefore, a high degree of reproducibility should be seen in comparative activities. The client's average variability between trials was 9.3%. This is indicative of an extremely consistent effort and the results are believed to indicate the client's maximum, safe level of performance. Mr. Vandermay passed the following validity criteria:

A. Average variability between comparative trials was less than 20%.
B. Majority of comparative lifts had variability less than 20%.
C. No single set of comparative lifts had variability in excess of 40%.
D. Fewer than two sets of comparative lifts had variability in excess of 30%.

Figure 6-3. Sample Narrative Report (*continues*)

2. **Hand Strength:** In Jamar, Position 2, right and left hand strengths were 120 and 125 pounds, respectively. Rapid Exchange Grips result in force measurements of approximately 110 pounds in each hand. With 10 repeated trials in Position 2 for phasic grip measurements, the last reading in the right hand was 110 pounds. The last reading in the left hand was 115 pounds. On the basis of these findings, the client has normal grip strengths and normal endurance.

3. **Pinch Strength:** Right and left hand Lateral Pinch strengths are 25 and 29 pounds, respectively.

4. **Standing:** The client is able to stand in an upright posture. There is forward head posture, but otherwise his standing posture is normal. Weight is borne approximately equally on both feet.

5. **Gait:** The client ambulates with a normal gait pattern. Heel strike and toe off are normal. Arm swing is normal. Stride lengths are equal.

6. **Squatting:** Mr. Vandermay is able to assume and arise from a deep squat posture. He was able to perform 10 repetitions of this activity, indicating that it caused his back pain to worsen somewhat.

7. **Kneeling:** The client is able to assume and maintain a tall kneeling posture. He is able to stay in this posture for one minute before asking to terminate the activity.

8. **Trunk Rotation:** The client was able to perform 10 complete trunk rotations standing and sitting. He reported this activity to be "painful."

9. **Balance Beam:** Prior to assessing a client on a balance beam, it is my protocol to first assess their ability to walk a straight line, keeping their feet on a line on the floor. The client is able to take part in this activity while walking forward. However, walking backward was performed in an incompetent fashion that precluded doing this portion of the assessment on a balance beam. **It is also noted that *unilateral balance* on each foot, with repeated measures, is approximately 15 seconds, which indicates a lack of balance/proprioceptive control.**

10. **Sitting:** The client sat in no apparent discomfort for 30 minutes while filling out paperwork and taking part in the intake interview. However, after that time, he arose periodically because of reported discomfort.

11. **Dynamic Pushing and Pulling:** The client is able to generate 20-25 pounds of force during pushing and pulling, both concentrically and eccentrically.

12. **Deferred Testing:** Heart rate was not monitored. The client is on blood pressure medication.

SECTION 9: LIMITING FACTORS AND FINAL OBSERVATIONS

1. **Limiting Factors for Material Handling Activities:** Lifting activities were terminated secondary to reported back pain. Given the high correlation between repeated measures, his subjective reports appear to be credible.

2. **Pain Reports and Behaviors During the FCE:** There were no overt pain behaviors of any kind noted during the clinical evaluation or the functional testing.

3. **Palpation and Visual Inspection:** There are two lateral incisions in the lumbar spine, each approximately 3 centimeters in length. There is a deep sulcus-like indentation between the incisions, most likely indicative of atrophy of the underlying musculature. The incisions are thin, well-heeled and have no apparent underlying adhesions. There is a midline incision anteriorly, approximately 20 centimeters in length. There are divots along the length of this relatively thick incision, possibly indicating underlying adhesions.

Figure 6-3. Sample Narrative Report (*continued*)

4. **Manual Strength Testing:** Manual testing produced the following results:

	Right	Left
Shoulder Flexion	5	5
Shoulder Abduction	5	5
Shoulder Adduction	5	5
Internal Rotation	5+	5+
External Rotation	5+	5+
Biceps Flexion	5+	5+
Triceps Extension	5+	5+
Wrist Flexion	5+	5+
Wrist Extension	5+	5+
Hip Adduction	5+	5+
Hip Abduction	5+	5+
Knee Flexion	5+	5+
Knee Extension	5+	5+
Dorsiflexion	5+	5+
Plantar Flexion	5+	5+
EHL	5+	5+

Please note that the measurements above are only semi-quantitative and that they represent the strengths found in the testing of isolated joints, as opposed to strengths demonstrated during functional activity. Manual test results do not necessarily correlate with functional abilities.

5. **Range of Motion Testing:** Active **cervical** ranges of motion appear below:

Flexion	45 degrees
Extension	70 degrees
Rotation	50 degrees bilaterally
Lateral Flexion	30 degrees bilaterally

Active **shoulder** ranges of motion appear below:

Flexion	160 degrees bilaterally
Abduction	160 degrees bilaterally
External Rotation	30 degrees bilaterally
Internal Rotation	Fingers to ~T6 bilaterally

Active **lumbar** ranges of motion appear below:

Flexion	60 degrees
Extension	<10 degrees
Rotation	20 degrees bilaterally
Lateral Flexion	15 degrees bilaterally

Straight leg raises appear below:

Right	45 degrees
Left	60 degrees

6. **Miscellaneous Testing and Observations:** Leg lengths are equal in the supine position. The ilial crests and ASIS are level when the client stands. There is equal excursion of the PSIS during lumbar flexion. Provocative testing fails to produce an asymmetry in the pelvic girdle. These findings indicate the client has apparent stability in the lumbar spine.

Figure 6-3. Sample Narrative Report (*continues*)

Dural stretch testing (supine position, non-painful straight leg raise followed by adduction of the leg past midline, internal rotation of the leg and dorsiflexion of the ankle) is negative bilaterally. The Slump Test (seated posture, followed by lumbar flexion and cervical flexion) is similarly negative. These findings indicate a likely absence of nerve root impingement in the lower lumbar spine.

Although ranges of motion are diminished in the lumbar spine, gross strengths throughout the body are within normal limits. All other ranges of motion are completely normal, as would be expected.

Per the results of the 90/90 Test, there is moderate tightness in the right hamstrings and significant tightness on the left side.

7. **Non-organic Signs:** None noted. The client was negative in all five Waddell categories.

Once again, thank you for referring Mr. Vandermay for evaluation. If I can be of further assistance, please contact me at your convenience.

Submitted by:

Darrell Schapmire, MS

Figure 6-3. Sample Narrative Report (*continued*)

CMS Policy

Centers for Medicare and Medicaid Services (CMS), a governmental agency that oversees the Medicare and Medicaid programs, has implemented guidelines regarding charges for missed appointments. They are as follows:

- Must not discriminate against Medicare beneficiaries, but also charge non-Medicare patients for missed appointments
- The amount the provider charges for the missed appointment must apply equally to all patients (Medicare and non-Medicare)
- Charges to beneficiaries for missed appointments should not be billed to Medicare

Medical Expert Witness

On occasion, a practicing physician may be hired as a medical expert witness, a medical expert who provides services from medical review through trial testimony in a lawsuit pertaining to:

- Medical malpractice
- Wrongful death
- Workers' compensation injury
- Motor vehicle injury
- Personal injury

Duties required by the physician as a medical expert witness may include:

- Consultation
- Case evaluation, including narrative reports
- A **deposition** (a statement under oath)
- Testimony

Range of Fees

Income generated from work performed as a medical expert witness varies by physician, specialty, and the number of cases the physician is involved in. The typical fee range is as follows:

- Research and consultation ($150.00–$250.00 per hour)
- Case review and preliminary evaluation ($400.00–$500.00 per hour)
- Narrative report ($150.00–$500.00)
- Depositions ($300.00–$500.00 per hour)
- Court and testimony ($200.00–$400.00 per hour)
- Travel time ($75.00 per hour average)

CHAPTER SUMMARY

- Medical offices can supplement their income by charging for administrative duties involving medical records copying, form completion, and narrative reports.
- A medical office must follow state laws regarding the allowed maximum amount for medical records copying.
- Most payers do not reimburse for CPT code 99080 – special reports; this fact justifies the rationale for charging patients for the time involved completing forms.
- If a medical office opts to charge for a missed appointment, the fee amount must be listed in the office's financial policy statement.
- A physician hired as a medical expert witness may charge for services including consultation, case evaluation, deposition(s), testimony and travel time.

REVIEW QUESTIONS

Short answer: Answer each question with a short statement.

1. How do administrative duties differ from clinical services in the medical office?

2. Who might request services pertaining to administrative duties?

3. What types of administrative requests may be made of the medical office?

4. How should a patient be notified for fees involving medical records copying?

5. List three types of form completion requests made of the medical office.

CODING BASICS

6. List three types of lawsuits a physician may be hired as a medical expert witness for.

7. What duties might a medical expert witness be required to perform?

8. What form is required when an entity requests a narrative report from the physician?

9. What is the typical fee range for a narrative report?

10. What is the CMS policy regarding missed appointment fees?

Chapter 7

Selecting an Outside Collection Agency

OBJECTIVES

Upon completion of this chapter, the student should be able to:

- Understand the role of a collection agency.
- Explain the factors in selecting a collection agency.
- Describe how collection agencies are paid.
- Discuss the importance of communications between the medical office and the collection agency.

KEY TERMS

Bonding

Contingency-fee

Delinquent

Errors and omissions insurance

Licensing

Surety bonds

THE ROLE OF A COLLECTION AGENCY

When in-office attempts at collecting have failed, medical offices may turn **delinquent** (past-due) accounts over to an outside collection agency. Medical offices vary in their decision of when it is necessary to transfer an account to collections; however, it is common to begin sending accounts once the patient has failed to make payments after three patient-due statements have been sent.

Selecting a Collection Agency

Medical offices may wish to consider several factors when choosing a collection agency. These might include:

- Credit worthiness
  - Verify banking references
  - Check credit report
- Insurance and **bonding** (the act of being protected against financial losses caused by a third party)
  - **Errors and omissions insurance** (insurance that protects a company from claims if a client holds the company responsible for errors, or the failure of workers to perform as promised in the contract)
- Employee dishonesty and **surety bonds** (promise of performance)
- **Licensing** (formal permission from a governmental or other constituted authority, as to carry on some business or profession)
  - The agency's licensing body as complaints against the agency would be made to this entity
- Experience with 'medical' collections

COLLECTION TECHNIQUES

All licensed collection agencies must follow the legal guidelines of the Fair Debt Collections Practice Act (FDCPA); however, it is important for medical offices to know the agency's techniques used in collecting. Questions to consider are:

- Does the agency send letters only, or use a combination of letters and telephone calls? See Figures 7-1 through 7-3.
- How many contacts will the agency make on an account?
- Does the agency sell its accounts or will uncollected accounts be returned to the medical office?

ABC Credit Services LLC
P.O. Box 12345
City, ST 67890

Date: April 21, 20YY

To: FirstName LastName
DebtorCompany
Address
City, State, ZIP

RE: Your account with:
Creditor
Address
City, State, ZIP

For the amount of $Amount
Phone: xxx-xxx-xxxx
Account ID: 1234567890

* * * * **COURTESY NOTICE** * * * *

The above client has requested that we contact you regarding the above referenced account. We realize that this amount due could be an oversight on your part and not a willful disregard of an apparent obligation.

Unless you notify this office within 30 days after receiving this notice that you dispute the validity of this debt or any portion thereof, this office will assume this debt is valid. If you notify this office in writing within 30 days from receiving this notice that you dispute the validity of this debt or any portion thereof, this office will obtain verification of the debt or obtain a copy of a judgment and mail you a copy of such judgment or verification. If you request this office in writing within 30 days after receiving this notice this office will provide you with the name and address of the original creditor, if different from the current creditor.

This communication is from a debt collector. **ABC Credit Services, LLC** is a collection agency attempting to collect a debt and any information obtained will be used for that purpose. Send correspondence, other than PAYMENTS, to this collection agency at P.O. Box 767095, City, ST 67890.

SEE REVERSE SIDE FOR IMPORTANT INFORMATION

*************************************** Detach and return with payment to ***************************************

Date: April 21, 20YY

Make check payable to: Creditor

Account ID: 1234567890

Amount Paid: ____________________

Mail payment to:

Home Phone: ____________________

Creditor
CreditorAddress
CreditorCity, State, ZIP

Please make any address corrections: Debtor Firstname Debtor Lastname
Debtor Address
Debtor City, State, ZIP

Figure 7-1. Sample courtesy notice letter from collection agency

ABC Credit Services LLC
P.O. Box 767095
City, ST 67890

Date: April 21, 20YY

To: FirstName LastName
DebtorCompany
Address
City, State, ZIP

RE: Your account with:
Creditor
Address
City, State, ZIP

For the amount of $Amount
Phone: xxx-xxx-xxxx
Account ID: 1234567890

*** * * * 2nd PAST DUE NOTICE * * * ***

Our client, **CREDITOR NAME,**
continues to show a past due balance on your account.

We are attempting to resolve this matter amicably; however, unless you forward payment to our client listed above, we will have no choice but to continue collection attempts.

This communication is from a debt collector. **ABC Credit Services, LLC** is a collection agency attempting to collect a debt and any information obtained will be used for that purpose. Send correspondence, other than PAYMENTS, to this collection agency at P.O. Box 767095, City, ST 67890.

SEE REVERSE SIDE FOR IMPORTANT INFORMATION

************************************** Detach and return with payment to **************************************

Make check payable to: Creditor

Account ID: 1234567890

Amount Paid: ____________________

Mail payment to:

Home Phone: ____________________

Creditor
Address
City, State, ZIP

Please make any address corrections:
Debtor Firstname Debtor Lastname
Debtor Address
Debtor City, State, ZIP

Figure 7-2. Sample second past-due notice letter from collection agency

ABC Credit Services LLC
P.O. Box 12345
City, ST

Date: April 21, 20YY

To: FirstName LastName
DebtorCompany
Address
City, State, ZIP

RE: Your account with:
Creditor
Address
City, State, ZIP

For the amount of $Amount
Phone: xxx-xxx-xxxx
Account ID: 1234567890

* * * * **FINAL NOTICE** * * * *

The statutory dispute period has expired. We are now permitted under Federal law to assume that this debt to **CREDITOR NAME** is valid.

Please make further collection efforts unnecessary by resolving this matter immediately.

This communication is from a debt collector. **ABC Credit Services, LLC** is a collection agency attempting to collect a debt and any information obtained will be used for that purpose. Send correspondence, other than PAYMENTS, to this collection agency at P.O. Box 767095, City, ST 67890.

SEE REVERSE SIDE FOR IMPORTANT INFORMATION

************************************** Detach and return with payment to **************************************

Make check payable to: Creditor

Account ID: 1234567890

Amount Paid: ____________________

Mail payment to:

Home Phone: ____________________

Creditor
Address
City, State, ZIP

Please make any address corrections:
Debtor Firstname Lastname
Debtor Address
Debtor City, State, ZIP

Figure 7-3. Sample final-notice letter from collection agency

COLLECTION AGENCY FEES

Most collection agencies work on a **contingency-fee** basis, which means the agency is paid their fee only when the account has been successfully paid. This fee is based on a percentage amount of the account debt. Typical fee range is between 15%–35%. For example, if a medical debt is $200, the agency's fee would range between $30–$70 on a successful collection of this debt.

THE IMPORTANCE OF COMMUNICATION

Communication between the medical office and the selected collection agency is imperative. Medical offices should inquire about how the collection agency intends to provide status reports of all assigned accounts. Questions for the medical office to consider asking the collection agency include:

- Will the agency provide reports to meet the medical office's needs?
- How often are reports generated—weekly, monthly, quarterly, or yearly?
- Is report generation and distribution included in the agency's fee, or is there an additional charge for this service?

Maintaining Customer Service

The same level of customer service that is expected of the medical office staff should extend to the collection agency environment. The medical office should make expectations for customer service known before signing a contract.

If the medical office continues to see patients who are in collections, and these patients have grievances over the collections agency's techniques, the grievances should be investigated, discussed, and handled in a way that is mutually acceptable by both parties.

CHAPTER SUMMARY

- When in-office collection attempts have failed, medical offices may hire an outside collection agency to collect on delinquent accounts.
- Several factors should be considered when selecting an outside collection agency. These include the agency's:
  - Credit worthiness
  - Insurance, bonding, and licensing
  - 'Medical' collections experience
  - Collection techniques
  - Fees for collecting
  - Method of reporting
- The medical office's expectations for customer service should extend beyond the office to include the level of service expected by the collection agency as well.

REVIEW QUESTIONS

Short answer: Answer each question with a short statement.

1. Why might a medical office seek the assistance of an outside collection agency?

2. Name three factors to be considered in selecting a collection agency.

3. What three questions should be asked of the collection agency regarding collection techniques?

4. How are collection agencies paid and what is their typical fee?

5. What three questions should be asked of the collection agency regarding their method of reporting?

6. How should patient grievances about the collection agency be handled?

Appendix I

Student Exercises

STOP AND PRACTICE

Exercise AI-1

Refer to the Medicare Remittance Advice form shown in Figure A-1 to answer the six questions in this exercise (the following list explains the column headers on the form).

- **Perf Prov**–Contains the performing provider's National Provider Identifier (NPI)
- **Serv Date**–Date services were rendered
- **POS**–Place of service
- **NOS**–Number of services
- **Proc**–Procedure code for service/s performed
- **Mods**–Modifiers
- **Billed**–The dollar amount billed for each service/procedure
- **Allowed**–The dollar amount Medicare allows for each service/procedure
- **Deduct**–If any portion of the claim was applied to the Medicare deductible, the dollar amount is listed here
- **Co-ins**–The dollar amount the patient is responsible to pay (usually 20%); if the patient has a supplemental insurance, Medicare forwards the claim to the said payer
- **Grp/RC-amt**–The dollar amount difference between the billed amount and the Medicare allowed amount; participating providers may not bill the patient for this amount
- **Prov Paid**–The dollar amount paid for the claim
- **Remark Codes**–Used as a reference for the status of a claim; explanation for denied claims are found here

1. How many providers rendered services?

2. Which patients should not receive patient statements for the claims listed on this Medicare Remittance Advice?

3. Why was Robert Breen's claim denied?

4. What action should the medical biller take regarding this claim?

5. Why was Joseph Edwards's claim denied?

6. What action should the medical biller take regarding this claim?

STOP AND PRACTICE

Exercise AI-2

Refer to the sample insurance aging report shown in Figure AI-2 to answer the following questions.

1. Which payer has the highest accounts receivable?

2. Which "days" column has the highest accounts receivable?

3. If the report date is May 5, 2008, how many claims are current?

4. Which patient has the oldest claim on this aging report?

Medicare Services
1Park Dr.
Harrisburg, PA 12345-0000
877-555-1234

Medicare Remittance Advice

Ocean Family Care
123 Ocean Lane
Ocean, NJ 00001

NPI #: 3355889955
Page 1 of 1
Date: 04/30/XX
Check/EFT# 229856

Perf Prov	Serv Date	POS	NOS	Proc Mods	Billed	Allowed	Deduct	Co-ins	Grp/RC-amt	Prov Paid
Name: Allens, Carole	HIC 112458974A			ACNT Allca000			ICN 020012459874		ASG Y	
1122336677	04122008	11	1	99205	200.00	172.50	0.00	34.50	CO-42 27.50	138.00
PT RESP	16.80			Claim totals	200.00	172.50	0.00	34.50	27.50	138.00 NET
Claim Info forwarded to: Cigna										
Name: Breen, Robert	HIC 154985698B1			ACNT Brero000			ICN 054125896525		ASG Y	
5544778800	04132008	11	1	99222	145.00	0.00	0.00	0.00	145.00-ZZ01	0.00
PT RESP	0.00			Claim totals	145.00	0.00	0.00	0.00	145.00	0.00 NET
Name: Cross, Mary	HIC 127632569B			ACNT Croma000			ICN 041257896523		ASG Y	
1122336677	04142008	11	1	99202	85.00	78.30	78.30	0.00	6.70	0.00
PT RESP	0.00			Claim totals	85.00	78.30	78.30	0.00	6.70	0.00 NET
Claim forwarded to: AARP										
Name: Davis, Susan	HIC 174824965A			ACNT Davsu000			ICN 092265489653		ASG Y	
9988665544	04122008	11	1	99245	225.00	0.00	0.00	0.00	225.00-MA130	0.00
PT RESP	0.00			Claim totals	225.00	0.00	0.00	0.00	225.00	0.00 NET
Name: Edwards, Joseph	HIC 223447623			ACNT Edwjo000			ICN 021458974562		ASG Y	
0066442233	04132008	11	1	81002	35.00	0.00	0.00	0.00	35.00-MA104	0.00
PT RESP	0.00			Claim totals	35.00	0.00	0.00	0.00	35.00	0.00 NET

Remark Codes:

MA104-HICnumber does not match our files
CO-42 Contractual Obligation
OA01-Other Primary Insurance
ZZ01-POS does not match CPT code
MA130-Refer phys NPI# missing

Figure AI-1. Sample Medicare Remittance Advice form

Insurance Company	0–30 Days	31–60 Days	61–90 Days	91+ Days
AETNA				
Allens, Lia ALLLI000 4/30/08 99213	$85.00			
Arthur, Sal ARTSA000 3/22/08 20610		$125.00		
Avery, Anne AVEAN000 12/10/07 69210				$80.00
Blue Cross/Blue Shield				
Blue, Betty BLUBO000 2/28/08 99204			$175.00	
Bray, Beth BRABE000 03/22/08 87070		$35.00		
Healthnet				
Crow, Cindy CROCI000 12/31/07 99205				$200.00
Medicare				
Dell, David DAVDI000 1/22/08 99213				$85.00
TRICARE				
Moore, Mary MOOMA000 4/27/08 99201	$50.00			
Morgan, Val MORGA000 4/05/08 69210	$80.00			

Figure AI-2: Sample insurance aging report

Appendix II

Forms, Lists, and Tables

After sending a physician notification form to site, and prior to sending the account to the outside agency, verify the following:

- ✓ See if patient has made contact within the last 14 days, by viewing financial and collection notes.
- ✓ Check patient registration form for obvious errors.
- ✓ Make sure there is no money attached to reversed charges.
- ✓ See if patient payments posted within the last 14 days.
- ✓ See if payment arrangements were set within the last 14 days.
- ✓ See if patient made contact or arrangements with site noted on the account.
- ✓ See if insurance contact was made or if any changes were made within the last 14 days.
- ✓ See if correspondence was received from patient indicating an update or change in responsibility.
- ✓ See if any overpayments exist on siblings account that can be moved and posted to bad debt account.

Figure AII-1. Collection agency checklist

1. **PREPARE:** Review the paperwork on the debtor before making the call. Know the history of the account, credit record, and the promises kept/broken. Have all records in front of you, ready for reference.
2. **ATTITUDE:** Adopt a strictly professional, business-like attitude. Remember, you have a contract, you delivered the goods, money is owed, and you have a right to expect payment. Never let it become personal. Don't yell or raise your voice; and NEVER swear. Don't threaten; legal action is your recourse unless you intend on carrying through with it.
3. **CONTACT:** Make sure you're talking to the right person.
4. **CONTROL:** Control the conversation. Keep it focused on the debt and on the repayment schedule. Don't let the patient sidetrack you with personal history, excuses, etc. Remember, the object of your call is to collect money, or to get a commitment, not to become friends with the customer or win arguments.
5. **FLEXIBLE:** Be ready to adjust to the situation. Think about the kind of patient you're dealing with and adapt to meet the circumstances. Be prepared to accept a reasonable payment schedule, and be willing to deal with a patient's circumstances.
6. **NOTES:** Keep detailed, accurate notes of every contact with the customer. Probe for further information on the customer. Notes of these contacts will help you in subsequent phone calls and may be invaluable in litigation. Good notes will also help in further credit decisions, or in cases where skip tracing may be needed.
7. **PRODUCTIVE:** Keep contact brief and to the point. This is a business call, not a social one. View your efforts on a ratio of time expended to results achieved. Long conversations probably mean the patient is stalling you, or trapping you in the "buddy syndrome."
8. **PRECISE:** Never leave a contact open ended, such as, "We'll talk next week," or "I'll send what I can." Every contact should result in a commitment to payment, of a specific amount, by a specific date, even the check number the customer is using to pay the pledge.
9. **TIME:** The longer an account is held, the less that will be recovered. If payment or a payout is not arranged within 90 days, place the claim with a collection agency or start legal proceedings.
10. **PLACEMENT:** Use this approach when you have decided that you are not going to be able to extract payment. It is in your best interest to immediately contact your collection agency of choice and place the account with them.

Figure AII-2. Ten Tips for successful collections

- Not being familiar with the FDCPA and unintentionally "harassing" a debtor
- Overlooking small balances
- Not taking action of NSF (non-sufficient funds) notices on bad checks
- Not using letters and forms to collect on past-due accounts
- Not training staff
- Not knowing how to set up realistic payment arrangements with parties
- Not asking for the money that is owed because the medical office does not like asking for money
- Waiting too long to use a collection agency

Figure AII-3. Common debt collection errors

State	Fee
Alabama	$30
Alaska	$30
Arizona	$25
Arkansas	$25
California	$25
Colorado	$20
Connecticut	$20
Delaware	$40
District of Columbia	$15
Florida	$25
Georgia	$30
Hawaii	$30
Idaho	$20
Illinois	$25
Indiana	$20
Iowa	$30
Kansas	$30
Kentucky	$25
Louisiana	$25
Maine	$25
Maryland	$35
Massachusetts	$25
Michigan	$25
Minnesota	$30
Mississippi	$30
Missouri	$40
Montana	$30
Nebraska	$30
Nevada	$25
New Hampshire	$25
New Jersey	$30
New Mexico	$25
New York	$20
North Carolina	$25
North Dakota	$25
Ohio	$30
Oklahoma	$25
Oregon	$25
Pennsylvania	$25
Rhode Island	$25
South Carolina	$30
South Dakota	$40
Tennessee	$30
Texas	$30
Utah	$20
Vermont	$25
Virginia	$35
Washington	$40
West Virginia	$25
Wisconsin	$25
Wyoming	$30

Figure AII-4. Non-sufficient funds check fees per state

Alabama

Section 12-21-6.1 Alabama Code Reproduction
The reasonable costs of reproducing copies of written or typed documents, or reports shall not be more than:

- $1 for each page of the first 25 pages.
- Not more than 50 cents for each page in excess of 25 pages.
- A search fee of $5.
- If the medical records are mailed to the person making the request, reasonable costs shall include the actual costs of mailing the medical records.
- In addition to the above fees, a person may charge the actual cost of reproducing X-rays and other special medical records.

Arizona

A.R.S. 12-2295

Except as otherwise provided by law, a healthcare provider or contractor may charge a person who requests copies of medical records a reasonable fee for the production of the records.

Except as necessary for continuity of care, a healthcare provider or contractor may require the payment of any fees in advance.

Arkansas

Arkansas Code Annotated [A.C.A.] Section 16-46-106

Medical clinics and doctors' offices:

- May charge no more than $5 for the first five pages.
- No more than 25 cents per page thereafter for existing records.
- Cost of each photocopy, excluding x-rays, shall not exceed $1 per page for the first five pages, and 25 cents for each additional page, except that the minimum charge shall be $5.

California Evidence Code Section 1560-1567

- Not more than 10 cents per page for 8.5 x 14 inches or less.
- 20 cents per page for microfilm copies.
- Actual costs for the reproduction of oversize documents or the reproduction of documents requiring special processing which are made in response to a subpoena.
- Reasonable clerical costs incurred in locating and making the records available to be billed at the maximum rate of $24 per hour per person, computed on the basis of $6 per quarter hour or fraction thereof.
- Actual postage charges.

Evidence Code Section 1158

If a patient's attorney requests the medical records:

- 10 cents per page for documents 8.5 x 14 inches or less.
- 20 cents per page for document copies from microfilm.
- Actual costs for oversize documents or special processing.
- Reasonable clerical costs to retrieve records; $4 per quarter hour or less.
- Actual postage charges.

Figure AII-5. Medical records copying fees by state (*continues*)

Colorado

6 C.C.R. 1011-1, Chapter 2, Part 5.2.3.4

- "Reasonable cost" not to exceed $14 for the first 10 or fewer pages.
- 50 cents per page for pages 11-40.
- 33 cents per page for every additional page.
- The per-page fee for records copied from microfilm shall be $1.50 per page.
- Actual postage or shipping costs and applicable sales tax, if any, may be charged.

Connecticut

Title 20 §20-7c(B)

Upon a written request of a patient, his attorney or authorized representative, or pursuant to a written authorization, a provider, except as provided in section 4-194, shall furnish to the person making such request a copy of the patient's health record, including but not limited to, bills, x-rays and copies of laboratory reports, contact lens specifications based on examinations and final contact lens fittings given within the preceding three months or such longer period of time as determined by the provider but no longer than six months, and records of prescriptions and other technical information used in assessing the patient's health condition. No provider shall charge more than:

- 45 cents per page, including any research fees, handling fees or related costs, and the cost of first class postage, if applicable.
- Except such provider may charge a patient the amount necessary to cover the cost of materials for furnishing a copy of an x-ray, provided no such charge shall be made for furnishing a health record or part thereof to a patient, his attorney or authorized representative if the record or part thereof is necessary for the purpose of supporting a claim or appeal under any provision of the Social Security Act and the request is accompanied by documentation of the claim or appeal.
- A provider shall furnish a health record requested pursuant to this section within 30 days of the request.

Section 19A-490B

Upon the written request of a patient or the patient's attorney or authorized representative, or pursuant to a written authorization, an institution licensed pursuant to this chapter shall furnish to the person making such request a copy of the patient's health record, including but not limited to, copies of bills, laboratory reports, prescriptions, and other technical information used in assessing the patient's health condition.

- No institution shall charge more than 65 cents per page, including any research fees, clerical fees, handling fees, or related costs, and the cost of first class postage.

Florida

Florida Statutes 395.3025

Rule 64B8-10.003, Florida Administrative Code

Regarding records from physicians:

- No more than $1 per page for the first 25 pages of written material.
- 25 cents for each additional page.
- Actual cost of reproducing nonwritten records such as x-rays.

Figure AII-5. Medical records copying fees by state

Georgia
Georgia General Assembly Unannotated Code §31-33-3
• A charge of up to $22.78 may be collected for search, retrieval, and other direct administrative costs.
• A fee for certifying the medical records may also be charged not to exceed $8.54 for each record certified.
• The actual cost of postage incurred in mailing the requested records may also be charged.
• Copying costs for a record which is in paper form shall not exceed:
  • 85 cents per page for the first 20 pages of the patient's records that are copied.
  • 74 cents per page for pages 21 through 100.
  • 57 cents for each page copied in excess of 100 pages.
  • These numbers reflect July 1, 2003 increase for inflation.
• For medical records that are not in paper form, including but not limited to radiology films, the provider shall be entitled to recover the full reasonable cost of such reproduction.

Hawaii Hawaii revised Statute Section 622-57(G) • Reasonable costs incurred by a healthcare provider in making copies of medical records shall be borne by the requesting person.
Illinois Illinois State CH 735 §5/8-2006 The practitioner shall be reimbursed by the person requesting such records at the time of such copying, for all reasonable expenses, including the costs of independent copy service companies, incurred by the practitioner in connection with such copying not to exceed: • A $22.28 handling charge for processing the request for copies. • 84 cents per page for pages 1 through 25. • 56 cents per page for pages 26 through 50. • 28 cents per page for all pages in excess of 50. • The charge shall not exceed $1.39 per page for any copies made from microfiche or microfilm. • Actual shipping costs. These rates shall be automatically adjusted as set forth in Section 8-2006. The physician or other practitioner may, however, charge for the reasonable cost of all duplication of record material or information that cannot routinely be copied or duplicated on a standard commercial photocopy machine such as x-ray films or pictures.

Figure AII-5. Medical records copying fees by state (*continues*)

Indiana IC 16-39-9-3: Charges Permitted for Providing Copies of Medical Records • (a) A provider may collect a charge of 25 cents per page for making and providing copies of medical records. If the provider collects a labor charge under subsection (b), the provider may not charge for making and providing copies of the first ten pages of a medical record under this subsection. • (b) A provider may collect a $15 labor charge in addition to the per-page charge collected under subsection (a). • (c) A provider may collect actual postage costs in addition to the charges collected under subsections (a) and (b). • (d) If the person requesting the copies requests that the copies be provided within two working days, and the provider provides the copies within two working days, the provider may collect a fee of $10 in addition to the charges collected under subsections (a) through (c).
Kansas K.S.A. 65-4971(B) • A fee for labor of $16.29. • 54 cents per page for first 250 pages. • 38 cents per page for additional pages. For copies of records that cannot be duplicated on a standard photocopy machine: "reasonable cost."
Kentucky KRS 422.317 Upon a patient's written request, a hospital licensed under KRS Chapter 216B or a healthcare provider shall provide, without charge to the patient, a copy of the patient's medical record. A copying fee, not to exceed $1 per page, may be charged by the healthcare provider for furnishing a second copy of the patient's medical record upon request either by the patient or the patient's attorney or the patient's authorized representative.
Louisiana Louisiana Revised Statutes 40:1299.96 For records, a reasonable charge not to exceed: • $1 per page for the first 25 pages. • 50 cents per page for pages 26-500. • 25 cents per page thereafter. • Plus handling charge of $15 for hospitals, $7.50 for other healthcare providers. • Plus actual postage. For x-rays, microfilm, electronic, and imaging media: • Reasonable reproduction costs. • Plus handling charge of $20 for hospitals, $10 for other healthcare providers.

Figure AII-5. Medical records copying fees by state

Maine

Title 22 Section 1711

- $10 for the first page.
- 35 cents for additional pages.

Maryland

Health-General Article Section 4-304(c)(3)

- Healthcare provider may charge a fee for copying and mailing not exceeding 50 cents for each page of the medical record. In addition to the fee charged under subparagraph (i) of this paragraph, a hospital or a healthcare provider may charge:
  - A preparation fee not to exceed $15 for medical record retrieval and preparation.
  - The actual cost for postage and handling of the medical record.
- This law, originally established in 1994, states that these fees may be adjusted annually for inflation in accordance with the Consumer Price Index.

Massachusetts

243 CMR 2.07(13)(c)

- A fee for copying in excess of 25 cents per page or a fee for clerical work in excess of $20 per hour is presumptively unreasonable.
- Charges for copies of x-rays and similar documents not reproducible by ordinary photocopying shall be at the licensee's actual cost, plus reasonable clerical fees not in excess of $20 per hour.

Michigan

Medical Records Access Act 47 of 2004 333.26269 Section 9 Fee:

- Initial fee of $20 per request for a copy of the record.
- Paper copies:
  - One dollar per page for the first 20 pages.
  - 50 cents per page for pages 21 through 50.
  - 20 cents for pages 51 and over.
- For mediums other than paper, the actual cost of copying.
- Postage or shipping costs.
- Actual costs incurred for records older than seven years.

Figure AII-5. Medical records copying fees by state (*continues*)

Minnesota

Minnesota Statute 144.335, Subdivision 5

When a provider or its representative makes copies of patient records upon a patient's request under this section, the provider or its representative may charge the patient or the patient's representative no more than:

- Seventy-five cents per page, plus $10 for time spent retrieving and copying the records, unless other law or a rule or contract provide for a lower maximum charge.
- This limitation does not apply to x-rays.
- The provider may charge a patient no more than the actual cost of reproducing x-rays, plus no more than $10 for the time spent retrieving and copying the x-rays.
- The respective maximum charges of 75 cents per page and $10 for time provided in this subdivision are in effect for calendar year 1992 and may be adjusted annually each calendar year as provided in this subdivision.

Mississippi

Section 11-1-52, Mississippi Code of 1972

- Maximum copying charge is $20 for up to 20 pages.
- $1 per page for the next 80 or more pages.
- 50 cents per page for all pages thereafter.
- 10% of the total charge may be added for postage and handling.
- $15 may be recovered by the medical provider or hospital or nursing home for retrieving medical records in archives at a location off the premises where the facility is located.
- Actual cost of reproducing x-rays or other special records.

Missouri

Missouri Revised Statutes §191.227

- A handling fee of $17.05, plus a fee of 40 cents per page for copies of documents made on a standard photocopy machine.
- Providers may charge for the reasonable cost of all duplications of medical record material or information that cannot routinely be copied or duplicated on a standard copy machine.

2005 Update

Provides that effective February 1 of each year, the handling fee and per page fee will be increased or decreased based on the annual percentage change in the unadjusted, U.S. city average, annual average inflation rate of the medical care component of the Consumer Price Index for all urban consumers. (CPI-U).

Montana

Montana Code Annotated 50-16-540

- A reasonable fee for providing healthcare information may not exceed 50 cents for each page for a paper copy or photocopy.
- A reasonable fee may include an administrative fee that may not exceed $15 for searching and handling recorded healthcare information.

Figure AII-5. Medical records copying fees by state

Nebraska

71-8404

- A provider may charge no more than $20 as a handling fee.
- No more than 50 cents per page as a copying fee.
- A provider may charge for the reasonable cost of all duplications of medical records that cannot routinely be copied or duplicated on a standard photocopy machine.
- A provider may charge an amount necessary to cover the cost of labor and materials for furnishing a copy of an x-ray or similar special medical record. If the provider does not have the ability to reproduce x-rays or other records requested, the person making the request may arrange, at his or her expense, for the reproduction of such records.

Nevada

NRS 629.061

- Actual cost of postage.
- Cost of making the copy, not to exceed 60 cents per page for photocopies and a reasonable cost for copies of x-ray photographs and other healthcare records produced by similar processes.
- No administrative fee or additional service fee of any kind may be charged for furnishing a copy.

New Hampshire

Title XXX Occupations and Professions Chapter 332-I Medical Records

- The charge for the copying of a patient's medical records shall not exceed $15 for the first 30 pages or 50 cents per page, whichever is greater.
- Copies of filmed records such as radiograms, x-rays, and sonograms shall be copied at a reasonable cost.

New Jersey

New Jersey Administrative Code §13:35G-6.5(c)(4)

Doctors: $1 per page or $100 for the whole record, whichever is less.

New Mexico

16.10.17 NMAC 16.10.17.8

Physicians must provide complete copies of medical records to a patient or to another physician in a timely manner when legally requested to do so by the patient or by a legally designated representative of the patient.

- A reasonable cost-based charge may be made for the cost of duplicating and mailing records.
- A reasonable charge is not more than $15 for the first 15 pages and 10 cents per page thereafter.
- Patients may be charged the actual cost of reproduction for electronic records and record formats other than paper, such as x-rays.

Sections 17 and 18 of Public Health Law (PHL), Laws of 1991, Chapter 165, Sections 48 and 49.

The cost can be no more than 75 cents per page for paper copies and a reasonable charge for diagnostic images, plus postage.

Figure AII-5. Medical records copying fees by state (*continues*)

North Carolina

North Carolina General Statutes §90-411

Inclusive of searching, handling, copying, and mailing costs:

- 75 cents for the first 25 pages.
- 50 cents for pages 26-100.
- 25 cents for pages over 100.
- Minimum fee of $10 permitted.

North Dakota

N.D. Cent. Code Section 23-12-14

Upon the request for medical records with the signed authorization of the patient, the healthcare provider shall provide medical records at a charge of no more than:

- $20 for the first 25 pages.
- 75 cents per page after 25 pages.
- This charge includes any administration fee, retrieval fee, and postage expense.

Ohio

[§3701.74.1] §3701.741.

Except as provided in divisions (C) and (E) of this section, a healthcare provider or medical records company that receives a request for a copy of a patient's medical record from the patient or patient's personal representative may charge not more than the amounts set forth in this section. Total costs for copies and all services related to those copies shall not exceed the sum of the following:

- $2.50 per page for the first 10 pages.
- 50 cents per page for pages 11 through 50.
- 20 cents per page for pages 51 and higher.
- With respect to data recorded other than on paper, $1.70 per page.
- The actual cost of any related postage incurred by the healthcare provider or medical records company.

Oklahoma

76 Oklahoma State Section 19

Any person who is or has been a patient of a doctor, hospital, or other medical institution shall be entitled, upon request, to obtain access to the information contained in the patient's medical records, including any x-ray or other photograph or image.

- The cost of each copy, not including any x-ray or other photograph or image, shall not exceed $1 for the first page and 50 cents for each subsequent page.
- The cost of each x-ray or other photograph or image shall not exceed $5 or the actual cost of reproduction, whichever is less.
- The physician, hospital, or other medical professionals and institutions may charge a patient for the actual cost of mailing the patient's requested medical records, but may not charge a fee for searching, retrieving, reviewing, and preparing medical records of the person.

Figure AII-5. Medical records copying fees by state

Oregon

ORS 192.521 Healthcare Provider and State Health Plan Charges

A healthcare provider or state health plan that receives an authorization to disclose protected health information may charge:

- No more than $25 for copying ten or fewer pages of written material and no more than 25 cents per page for each additional page.
- Postage costs to mail copies of protected health information or an explanation or summary of protected health information, if requested by an individual or a personal representative of the individual.
- Actual costs of preparing an explanation or summary of protected health information, if requested by an individual or a personal representative of the individual.

Pennsylvania

Act 26 of 2006

Act 26 sets the maximum fees that can be charged for medical records. These fees are updated yearly through the Department of Health. With a few exceptions, the maximum fees for a record request from a patient or attorney for 2007 are as follows:

- Searching and retrieving the record - $18.54.
- Pages 1 through 20 - $1.25 per page.
- Pages 21 through 60 - 93 cents per page.
- Pages 61 and after - 31 cents per page.
- Copies from microfilm - $1.68.
- Actual mailing or delivery fees.

Rhode Island

Rules and Regulations for the Licensure and Discipline of Physicians §11.2

- Not more than 25 cents per page for the first 100 pages.
- After 100 pages, not more than 10 cents per page.
- Maximum fee of $15 for retrieval regardless of time spent retrieving.
- Special handling fee of an additional $10 if records must be delivered within 48 hours of request.
- Copying of x-rays or other documents not reproducible by photocopy at physician's actual cost plus clerical fees not to exceed $15.

South Carolina

South Carolina State Section 44-115-80

A physician or other owner of medical records may charge a fee for the search and duplication of a medical record, but the fee may not exceed:

- 65 cents per page for the first 30 pages.
- 50 cents per page for all other pages.
- A clerical fee for searching and handling not to exceed $15 per request.
- Plus actual postage and applicable sales tax.
- The physician may charge no more than the actual cost of reproduction of an x-ray.

Figure AII-5. Medical records copying fees by state (*continues*)

South Dakota

South Dakota Codified Laws Section 34-12-15

A healthcare facility shall provide copies of all medical records, reports, and x-rays pertinent to the health of the patient, if available, to a discharged patient or the patient's designee upon receipt by the healthcare facility of a written request or a legible copy of a written request signed by the patient. The healthcare facility may require before delivery that the patient pay the actual reproduction and mailing expense.

Tennessee

Tennessee Code/Title 63 Professions of the Healing Arts/Chapter 2 Medical Records/63-2-102

- For other than records involving workers' compensation cases, such reasonable costs shall not exceed $20 for medical records 40 pages or less in length.
- 25 cents per page for each page copied after the first 40 pages.
- The actual cost of mailing.

Texas

22 Texas Administrative Code §165.2(E)

Doctors: No more than $25.00 for the first 20 pages; then,

- 50 cents per page for every copy thereafter.
- In addition, actual cost of mailing or shipping.
- Also, a reasonable fee not to exceed $15 for executing affidavit.

22 Texas Administrative Code §165.3

Doctors: Maximum charge for x-rays and diagnostic imaging studies $8 per copy.

Vermont

18 V.S.A. §9419. Charges for Access to Medical Records:

- A custodian may impose a charge that is no more than a flat $5 fee or no more than 50 cents per page, whichever is greater, for providing copies of an individual's healthcare record.
- A custodian may charge an individual a fee, reasonably related to the associated costs, for providing copies of x-rays, films, models, disks, tapes, or other healthcare record information maintained in other formats.

Virginia

Virginia Code Section 8.01-413 (2003)

A reasonable charge may be made for the service of maintaining, retrieving, reviewing and preparing such copies. Except for copies of x-ray photographs, however, such charges shall not exceed:

- 50 cents per page for up to 50 pages.
- 25 cents per page thereafter for copies from paper or other hard copy generated from computerized or other electronic storage, or other photographic, mechanical, electronic, imaging or chemical storage process.

Figure AII-5. Medical records copying fees by state

Virginia *(continued)*

- $1 per page for copies from microfilm or other micrographic process plus all postage and shipping costs and a search and handling fee not to exceed $10.00.
- Copies of hospital, nursing facility, physician's, or other healthcare provider's records or papers shall be furnished within 15 days of such request.

Virginia Code §32.1-127.1:03. Health Records

If an individual or his agent/attorney requests a copy of his own medical records, the healthcare entity may impose a reasonable cost-based fee, which shall include the cost of supplies for and labor of copying the requested information, as well as postage where applicable.

Washington

WAC 246-08-400

- No more than 88 cents per page for the first 30 pages.
- No more than 67 cents per page for all other pages.
- The provider can charge a $20 clerical fee for searching and handling records.
- If the provider personally edits confidential information from the record, as required by statute, the provider can charge the usual fee for a basic office visit.
- This section is effective July 1, 2003, through June 30, 2005.

West Virginia

West Virginia Code §16-29-2(A)

- A $10 maximum search fee plus "reasonable expenses" provided that the cost may not exceed 75 cents per page for copying of records already reduced to written form.

Wisconsin

Wisconsin Chapter HFS 117.05

If a patient or if the personal representative of the patient requests copies of the patient's healthcare records, the healthcare provider may charge no more than the following fees:

- 31 cents per record page.
- For x-rays, $5.25 per x-ray copy.
- Actual costs of postage or other means of delivering the requested duplicate records to the attorney.
- Sales taxes, if applicable, also may be added to the fees charged under this subsection.

Wyoming

Wyoming Statutes Title 35, Chapter 2, Article 6, Section 35-2-611(B)

The hospital may charge a reasonable fee, not to exceed the hospital's actual cost, for providing the healthcare information and is not required to permit examination or copying until the fee is paid.

Figure AII-5. Medical records copying fees by state

Alabama Alabama Department of Insurance 201 Monroe Street, Suite 1700 Montgomery, Alabama 36104 Phone: 334.269.3550 Fax: 334.241.4192 http://www.aldoi.gov/
Alaska Alaska Division of Insurance 550 West 7th Avenue, Suite 1560 Anchorage, Alaska 99501-3567 Phone: 907.269.7900 Fax: 907.269.7910 http://www.deed.state.ak.us/insurance/
Arizona Arizona Department of Insurance 2910 North 44th Street, Suite 210 Phoenix, Arizona 85018-7256 Phone: 602.912.8400 Fax: 602.912.8452 http://www.id.state.az.us/
Arkansas Arkansas Department of Insurance 1200 West 3rd Street Little Rock, Arkansas 72201-1904 Phone: 501.371.2600 Fax: 501.371.2629 http://insurance.arkansas.gov/

Figure AII-6. Department of Insurance by state

California California Department of Insurance 300 Capital Mall, Suite 1700 Sacramento, California 95814 Phone: 916.492.3500 Fax: 916.445.5280 http://www.insurance.ca.gov/
Colorado Colorado Division of Insurance 1560 Broadway, Suite 850 Denver, Colorado 80202 Phone: 303.894.7499 Fax: 303.894.7455 http://www.dora.state.co.us/insurance/
Connecticut Connecticut Department of Insurance P.O. Box 816 Hartford, Connecticut 06142-0816 Phone: 860.297.3800 Fax: 860.566.7410 (Street Address: 153 Market Street, 7th Floor, Hartford, Connecticut 06103) http://www.ct.gov/cid/site/default.asp
Delaware Delaware Department of Insurance Rodney Building 841 Silver Lake Boulevard Dover, Delaware 19904 Phone: 302.739.4251 Fax: 302.739.5280 http://www.state.de.us/inscom/default.shtml

Figure AII-6. Department of Insurance by state (*continues*)

District of Columbia Department of Insurance, Securities Regulation and Banking Government of the District of Columbia 810 First Street, N.E. Suite 701 Washington, DC 20002 Phone: 202.727.8000 Fax: 202.535.1196 http://disr.washingtondc.gov/disr/site/default.asp
Florida Office of Insurance Regulation Florida Department of Financial Services State of Florida 200 East Gaines Street, Room 101A Tallahassee, Florida 32399-0301 Phone: 850.413.5914 Fax: 850.488.3334 http://www.floir.com/
Georgia Georgia Department of Insurance 2 Martin Luther King, Jr. Drive Floyd Memorial Building 704 West Tower Atlanta, Georgia 30334 Phone: 404.656.2056 Fax: 404.657.7493 http://www.gainsurance.org

Figure AII-6. Department of Insurance by state

Hawaii
Hawaii Insurance Division
Department of Commerce & Consumer Affairs
P.O. Box 3614
Honolulu, Hawaii 96811-3614
Phone: 808-586.2790
Fax: 808.586.2806
(Street Address: 335 Merchant Street, Room 213, Honolulu, Hawaii 96813)
http://www.hawaii.gov/dcca/areas/ins/
Idaho
Idaho Department of Insurance
700 West State Street, 3rd Floor
Boise, Idaho 83720-0043
Phone: 208.334.4250
Fax: 208.334.4398
http://www.doi.idaho.gov/
Illinois
Department of Financial and Professional Regulation
Illinois Division of Insurance
100 West Randolph Street, Suite 9-301
Chicago, Illinois 60601-3251
Phone: 312.814.2427
Fax: 312.814.5435
http://www.idfpr.com/DOI/Default2.asp
Indiana
Indiana Department of Insurance
311 W. Washington Street, Suite 300
Indianapolis, Indiana 46204-2787
Phone: 317.232.2385
Fax: 317.232.5251
http://www.ai.org/idoi/index.html

Figure AII-6. Department of Insurance by state (*continues*)

Iowa
Division of Insurance State of Iowa 330 E. Maple Street Des Moines, Iowa 50319 Phone: 515.281.5523 Fax: 515.281.3059 http://www.iid.state.ia.us/
Kansas
Kansas Department of Insurance 420 S.W. 9th Street Topeka, Kansas 66612-1678 Phone: 785.296.3071 Fax: 785.296.7805 http://www.ksinsurance.org/
Kentucky
Kentucky Office of Insurance P.O. Box 517 Frankfort, Kentucky 40602-0517 Phone: 502.564.6027 Fax: 502.564-1453 (Street Address: 215 West Main Street, Frankfort, Kentucky 40601) http://doi.ppr.ky.gov/kentucky/
Louisiana
Louisiana Department of Insurance P.O. Box 94214 Baton Rouge, Louisiana 70804-9214 Phone: 225.342.5423 Fax: 225.342.8622 (Street Address: 1702 N. 3rd Street, Baton Rouge, Louisiana 70802) http://www.ldi.state.la.us/

Figure AII-6. Department of Insurance by state

Maine Maine Bureau of Insurance Department of Professional & Financial Regulation State Office Building, Station 34 Augusta, Maine 04333-0034 Phone: 207.624.8475 Fax: 207.624.8599 (Street Address: 124 Northern Avenue, Gardiner, Maine 04345) http://www.state.me.us/pfr/ins/ins_index.htm
Maryland Maryland Insurance Administration 525 St. Paul Place Baltimore, Maryland 21202-2272 Phone: 410.468.2090 Fax: 410.468.2020 http://www.mdinsurance.state.md.us/
Massachusetts Division of Insurance Commonwealth of Massachusetts One South Station, 5th Floor Boston, Massachusetts 02110 Phone: 617.521.7794 Fax: 617.521.7758 http://www.mass.gov/doi
Michigan Office of Financial and Insurance Services Attention: Office of the Commissioner P.O. Box 30220 Lansing, Michigan 48909 Phone: 517.373.0220 Fax: 517.373.4870 (Street Address: Ottawa Building, 3rd Floor, 611 W. Ottawa, Lansing, Michigan 48913) http://www.michigan.gov/cis/0,1607,7-154-10555---,00.html

Figure AII-6. Department of Insurance by state (*continues*)

Minnesota Minnesota Department of Commerce 85 7th Place, East, Suite 500 St. Paul, Minnesota 55101-2198 Phone: 651-296-4026 Fax: 651.282.2568 http://www.state.mn.us/portal/mn/jsp/home.do?agency=Commerce
Mississippi Mississippi Insurance Department P.O. Box 79 Jackson, Mississippi 39205 Phone: 601.359.3569 Fax: 601.359.2474 (Street Address: 501 North West Street, 10th Floor, Jackson, Mississippi 39201) http://www.doi.state.ms.us/
Missouri Missouri Department of Insurance 301 West High Street, Suite 530 Jefferson City, Missouri 65102 Phone: 573.751.4126 Fax: 573.751.1165 http://www.insurance.mo.gov/
Montana Montana Department of Insurance 840 Helena Avenue Helena, Montana 59601 Phone: 406.444.2040 Fax: 406.444.3497 http://sao.mt.gov/

Figure AII-6. Department of Insurance by state

Nebraska Nebraska Department of Insurance Terminal Building, Suite 400 941 'O' Street Lincoln, Nebraska 68508 Phone: 402.471.2201 Fax: 402.471.4610 http://www.doe.ne.gov/
Nevada Nevada Division of Insurance 788 Fairview Drive, Suite 300 Carson City, Nevada 89701-5753 Phone: 775.687.4270 Fax: 775.687.3937 http://doi.state.nv.us/
New Hampshire New Hampshire Insurance Department 21 South Fruit Street, Suite 14 Concord, New Hampshire 03301 Phone: 603.271.2261 Fax: 603.271.1406 http://www.state.nh.us/insurance/
New Jersey New Jersey Department of Insurance 20 West State Street, CN 325 Trenton, New Jersey 08625 Phone: 609.292.5360 Fax: 609.984.5273 http://www.state.nj.us/dobi/index.shtml

Figure AII-6. Department of Insurance by state (*continues*)

New Mexico New Mexico Department of Insurance P.O. Drawer 1269 Santa Fe, New Mexico 87504-1269 Phone: 505.827.4601 Fax: 505.476.0326 (Street Address: PERA Building, 1120 Paseo de Peralta, Santa Fe, New Mexico 87501) http://www.nmprc.state.nm.us/insurance/inshm.htm
New York New York Department of Insurance 25 Beaver Street New York, New York 10004-2319 Phone: 212.480.2289 Fax: 212.480.2310 OR New York Department of Insurance One Commerce Plaza, Suite 1700 Albany, New York 12257 Phone: 518.474.4567 Fax: 518.473.4139 http://www.ins.state.ny.us/
North Carolina Department of Insurance State of North Carolina 1201 Mail Service Center Raleigh, North Carolina 27699-1201 Phone: 919.733.3058 Fax: 919.733.6495 (Street Address: Dobbs Building, 430 N. Salisbury Street, Raleigh, North Carolina 27603) http://www.ncdoi.com/

Figure AII-6. Department of Insurance by state

North Dakota North Dakota Department of Insurance 600 E. Boulevard Bismark, North Dakota 58505-0320 Phone: 701.328.2440 Fax: 701.328.4880 http://www.state.nd.us/ndins/
Ohio Ohio Department of Insurance 2100 Stella Court Columbus, Ohio 43215-1067 Phone: 614.644.2658 Fax: 614.644.3743 http://www.ohioinsurance.gov/
Oklahoma Oklahoma Department of Insurance 2401 NW 23rd Street, Suite 28 Oklahoma City, Oklahoma 73107 Phone: 405.521.2828 Fax: 405.521.6635 http://www.oid.state.ok.us/
Oregon Oregon Insurance Division P.O. Box 14480 Salem, Oregon 97309-0405 Phone: 503.947.7980 Fax: 503.378.4351 Street Address: 350 Winter Street NE, Room 440, Salem, OR 97301-3883) http://www.cbs.state.or.us/external/ins/index.html

Figure AII-6. Department of Insurance by state (*continues*)

Pennsylvania Pennsylvania Insurance Department 1326 Strawberry Square, 13th Floor Harrisburg, Pennsylvania 17120 Phone: 717.783.0442 Fax: 717.772.1969 http://www.ins.state.pa.us/ins/site/default.asp
Puerto Rico Puerto Rico Department of Insurance P.O. Box 8330 – Fernandez Juncos Station Santurce, Puerto Rico 00910-8330 Phone: 787.722.8686 Fax: 787.722.4400 Street Address: Puerto Rico Department of Insurance Cobian's Plaza Building 1607 Ponce de Leon Avenue Stop 23 Fernandez Juncos Station Santurce, Puerto Rico 00909 http://www.gobierno.pr/GPRPortal/Inicio/EconomiayComercio/Seguros.htm
Rhode Island Rhode Island Insurance Division Department of Business Regulation 233 Richmond Street, Suite 233 Providence, Rhode Island 02903-4233 Phone: 401.222.5466 Fax: 401.222.5475 http://www.dbr.state.ri.us/

Figure AII-6. Department of Insurance by state

South Carolina
South Carolina Department of Insurance P.O. Box 100105 Columbia, South Carolina 29202-3105 Phone: 803.737.6212 Fax: 803.737.6229 (Street Address: 300 Arbor Lake Drive, Suite 1200, Columbia, South Carolina 29223) http://www.doi.sc.gov/
South Dakota South Dakota Division of Insurance Department of Revenue and Regulation 445 East Capital Avenue, 1st Floor Pierre, South Dakota 57501-3185 Phone: 605.773.4104 Fax: 605.773.5369 http://www.state.sd.us/drr2/reg/insurance/
Tennessee Tennessee Department of Commerce & Insurance Davy Crockett Tower, 5th Floor 500 James Robertson Parkway Nashville, Tennessee 37243-0565 Phone 615.741.6007 Fax: 615.532.6934 http://www.state.tn.us/commerce/insurance/index.html
Texas Texas Department of Insurance P.O. Box 149104 Austin, Texas 78714-9104 Phone: 512.463.6464 Fax: 512.475.2005 (Street Address: 333 Guadalupe Street, Austin, Texas 78701) http://www.tdi.state.tx.us/

Figure AII-6. Department of Insurance by state (*continues*)

Utah Department of Insurance 3110 State Office Building Salt Lake City, Utah 84114-1201 Phone: 801.538.3800 Fax: 801.538.3829 http://www.insurance.utah.gov/
Vermont Vermont Division of Insurance Department of Banking, Insurance & Securities 89 Main Street, Drawer 20 Montpelier, Vermont 05620-3101 Phone: 802.828.3301 Fax: 802.828.3306 http://www.bishca.state.vt.us/
Virginia State Corporation Commission Bureau of Insurance Commonwealth of Virginia P.O. Box 1157 Richmond, Virginia 23218 Phone: 804.371.9694 Fax: 804.371.9873 (Street Address: 1300 East Main Street, Richmond, Virginia 23219) http://www.scc.virginia.gov/division/boi/index.htm
Washington Washington State Office of the Insurance Commissioner P.O. Box 40255 Olympia, Washington 98504-0255 Phone: 360.725.7000 Fax: 360.586.3109 (Street Address: Insurance 5000 Building, 5000 Capital Way, Tumwater, Washington 98501) http://www.insurance.wa.gov/

Figure AII-6. Department of Insurance by state

West Virginia West Virginia Department of Insurance P.O. Box 50540 Charleston, West Virginia 25305-0540 Phone: 304.558.3354 Fax: 304.558.0412 (Street Address: 1124 Smith Street, Charleston West Virginia 25301) http://www.wvinsurance.gov/
Wisconsin Office of the Commissioner of Insurance State of Wisconsin P.O. Box 7873 Madison, Wisconsin 53707-7873 Phone: 608.267.1233 Fax: 608.261.8579 (Street Address: 125 South Webster Street, GEF III – 2nd Floor, Madison, Wisconsin 53702) http://oci.wi.gov/
Wyoming Wyoming Department of Insurance Herschler Building 122 West 25th Street, 3rd East Cheyenne, Wyoming 82002-0440 Phone: 307.777.7401 Fax: 307.777.5895 http://insurance.state.wy.us/

Figure AII-6: Department of Insurance by state

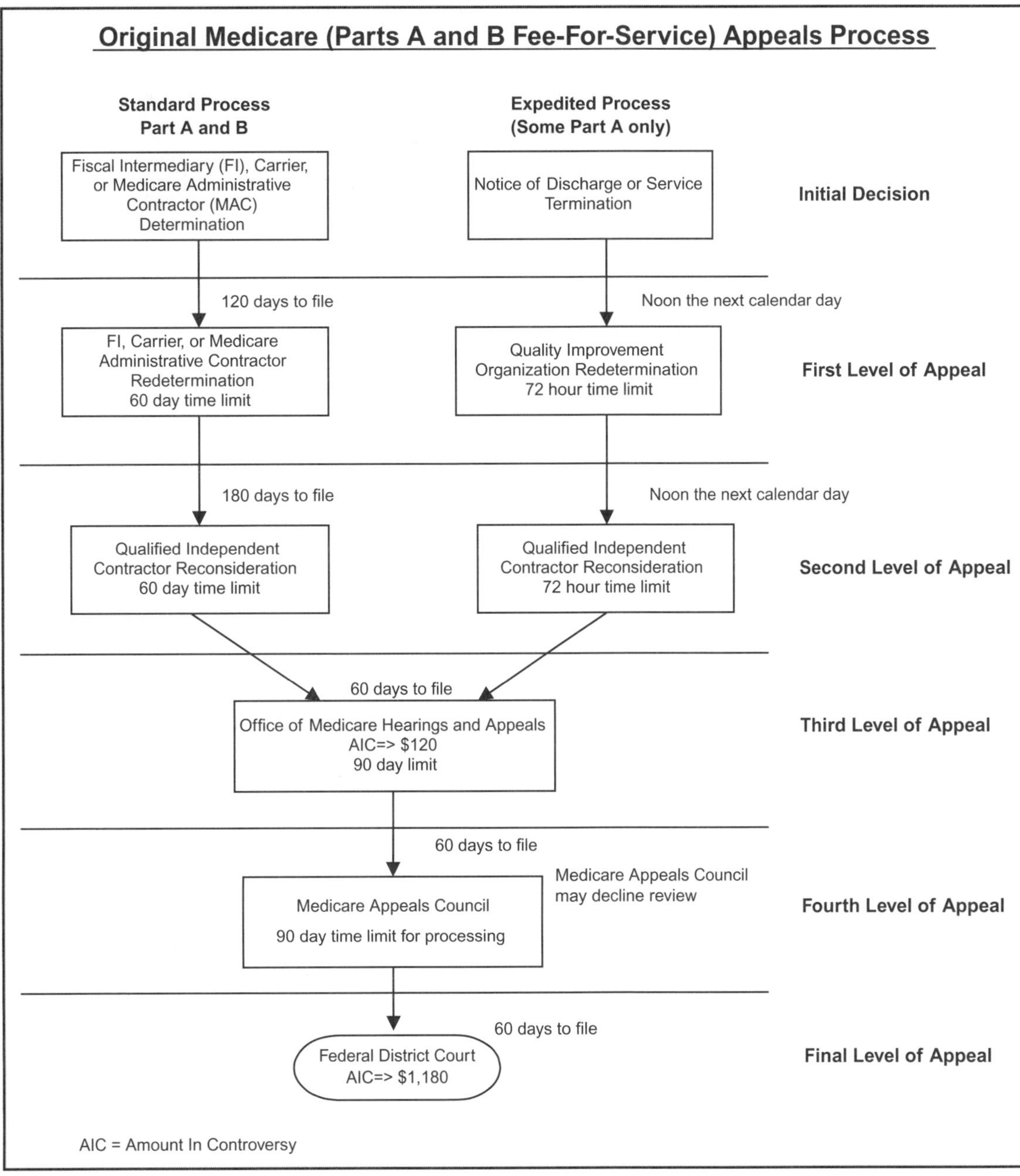
Original Medicare (Parts A and B Fee-For-Service) Appeals Process
Standard Process
Part A and B
Expedited Process
(Some Part A only)
Fiscal Intermediary (FI), Carrier, or Medicare Administrative Contractor (MAC) Determination
Notice of Discharge or Service Termination
Initial Decision
120 days to file
Noon the next calendar day
FI, Carrier, or Medicare Administrative Contractor Redetermination
60 day time limit
Quality Improvement Organization Redetermination
72 hour time limit
First Level of Appeal
180 days to file
Noon the next calendar day
Qualified Independent Contractor Reconsideration
60 day time limit
Qualified Independent Contractor Reconsideration
72 hour time limit
Second Level of Appeal
60 days to file
Office of Medicare Hearings and Appeals
AIC=> $120
90 day limit
Third Level of Appeal
60 days to file
Medicare Appeals Council
90 day time limit for processing
Medicare Appeals Council may decline review
Fourth Level of Appeal
60 days to file
Federal District Court
AIC=> $1,180
Final Level of Appeal
AIC = Amount In Controversy

Figure AII-7. Original Medicare appeal process

(*A*) **Notifier(s):**

(*B*) **Patient Name:** (*C*) **Identification Number:**

ADVANCE BENEFICIARY NOTICE OF NONCOVERAGE (ABN)

NOTE: If Medicare doesn't pay for (*D*)_______________ below, you may have to pay.

Medicare does not pay for everything, even some care that you or your health care provider have good reason to think you need. We expect Medicare may not pay for the (*D*) _______________ below.

(*D*) _______________	(*E*) **Reason Medicare May Not Pay:**	(*F*) **Estimated Cost:**

WHAT YOU NEED TO DO NOW:

- Read this notice, so you can make an informed decision about your care.
- Ask us any questions that you may have after you finish reading.
- Choose an option below about whether to receive the (*D*) _______________ listed above.

  Note: If you choose Option 1 or 2, we may help you to use any other insurance that you might have, but Medicare cannot require us to do this.

(*G*) **OPTIONS:** **Check only one box. We cannot choose a box for you.**
❑ **OPTION 1.** I want the (*D*) _______________ listed above. You may ask to be paid now, but I also want Medicare billed for an official decision on payment, which is sent to me on a Medicare Summary Notice (MSN). I understand that if Medicare doesn't pay, I am responsible for payment, but **I can appeal to Medicare** by following the directions on the MSN. If Medicare does pay, you will refund any payments I made to you, less co-pays or deductibles.
❑ **OPTION 2.** I want the (*D*) _______________ listed above, but do not bill Medicare. You may ask to be paid now as I am responsible for payment. **I cannot appeal if Medicare is not billed.**
❑ **OPTION 3.** I don't want the (*D*) _______________ listed above. I understand with this choice I am **not** responsible for payment, and **I cannot appeal to see if Medicare would pay.**

(*H*) **Additional Information:**

This notice gives our opinion, not an official Medicare decision. If you have other questions on this notice or Medicare billing, call **1-800-MEDICARE** 1-800-633-4227/**TTY**: 1-877-486-2048).

Signing below means that you have received and understand this notice. You also receive a copy.

(*I*) **Signature:**	(*J*) **Date:**

According to the Paperwork Reduction Act of 1995, no persons are required to respond to a collection of information unless it displays a valid OMB control number. The valid OMB control number for this information collections is 0938-0566. The time required to complete this information collections is estimated to average 7 minutes per response, including the time to review instructions, search existing data resources, gather the data needed, and complete and review the information collections. If you have comments concerning the accuracy of the time estimate or suggestions for improving this form, please write to: CMS, 7500 Security Boulevard, Attn: PRA Reports Clearance Officer, Baltimore, Maryland 21244-1850.

Form CMS-R-131 (03/08) Form Approved OMB No, 0938-0566

Figure AII-8. The Advance Beneficiary Notice (ABN)

Appendix III

CMS-1500 Claim Filing Instructions

BLOCKS 1–13: PATIENT AND INSURED INFORMATION

Block 1: Check the medical payer type for the claim by marking an "X" in the appropriate box.

- Options are MEDICARE, MEDICAID, TRICARE CHAMPUS, CHAMPVA, GROUP HEALTH PLAN, FECA BLK LUNG, and OTHER.
- The OTHER box can include HMO, commercial, motor vehicle, liability, or workers' compensation insurance.

Block 2: Enter the patient's full legal name, beginning with the last name, then first name and middle initial.

- Insert a comma between the last name and first name and before the middle initial.
- If patient's last name includes a suffix (e.g., Jr. or Sr.), enter the suffix after the last name.
- Do not enter professional credentials or designations (e.g., M.D., Esq.) in this box.
- A hyphen may be inserted for hyphenated last names.
- Do not enter a period in this block.

1500

HEALTH INSURANCE CLAIM FORM

APPROVED BY NATIONAL UNIFORM CLAIM COMMITTEE 08/05

PICA | PICA

CARRIER

1. MEDICARE (Medicare #) MEDICAID (Medicaid #) TRICARE CHAMPUS (Sponsor's SSN) CHAMPVA (Member ID#) GROUP HEALTH PLAN (SSN or ID) FECA BLK LUNG (SSN) OTHER (ID)
1a. INSURED'S I.D. NUMBER (For Program in Item 1)

2. PATIENT'S NAME (Last Name, First Name, Middle Initial)
3. PATIENT'S BIRTH DATE MM DD YY SEX M F
4. INSURED'S NAME (Last Name, First Name, Middle Initial)

5. PATIENT'S ADDRESS (No., Street)
6. PATIENT RELATIONSHIP TO INSURED Self Spouse Child Other
7. INSURED'S ADDRESS (No., Street)

CITY STATE
8. PATIENT STATUS Single Married Other
CITY STATE

ZIP CODE TELEPHONE (Include Area Code) ( )
Employed Full-Time Student Part-Time Student
ZIP CODE TELEPHONE (Include Area Code) ( )

9. OTHER INSURED'S NAME (Last Name, First Name, Middle Initial)
10. IS PATIENT'S CONDITION RELATED TO:
11. INSURED'S POLICY GROUP OR FECA NUMBER

a. OTHER INSURED'S POLICY OR GROUP NUMBER
a. EMPLOYMENT? (Current or Previous) YES NO
a. INSURED'S DATE OF BIRTH MM DD YY SEX M F

b. OTHER INSURED'S DATE OF BIRTH MM DD YY SEX M F
b. AUTO ACCIDENT? YES NO PLACE (State)
b. EMPLOYER'S NAME OR SCHOOL NAME

c. EMPLOYER'S NAME OR SCHOOL NAME
c. OTHER ACCIDENT? YES NO
c. INSURANCE PLAN NAME OR PROGRAM NAME

d. INSURANCE PLAN NAME OR PROGRAM NAME
10d. RESERVED FOR LOCAL USE
d. IS THERE ANOTHER HEALTH BENEFIT PLAN? YES NO *If yes*, return to and complete item 9 a-d.

READ BACK OF FORM BEFORE COMPLETING & SIGNING THIS FORM.

12. PATIENT'S OR AUTHORIZED PERSON'S SIGNATURE I authorize the release of any medical or other information necessary to process this claim. I also request payment of government benefits either to myself or to the party who accepts assignment below.

SIGNED ____ DATE ____

13. INSURED'S OR AUTHORIZED PERSON'S SIGNATURE I authorize payment of medical benefits to the undersigned physician or supplier for services described below.

SIGNED ____

PATIENT AND INSURED INFORMATION

14. DATE OF CURRENT: MM DD YY ILLNESS (First symptom) OR INJURY (Accident) OR PREGNANCY(LMP)
15. IF PATIENT HAS HAD SAME OR SIMILAR ILLNESS. GIVE FIRST DATE MM DD YY
16. DATES PATIENT UNABLE TO WORK IN CURRENT OCCUPATION MM DD YY FROM TO MM DD YY

17. NAME OF REFERRING PROVIDER OR OTHER SOURCE 17a. 17b. NPI
18. HOSPITALIZATION DATES RELATED TO CURRENT SERVICES MM DD YY FROM TO MM DD YY

19. RESERVED FOR LOCAL USE
20. OUTSIDE LAB? YES NO $ CHARGES

21. DIAGNOSIS OR NATURE OF ILLNESS OR INJURY (Relate Items 1, 2, 3 or 4 to Item 24E by Line)

1. ___ . ___ 3. ___ . ___

2. ___ . ___ 4. ___ . ___

22. MEDICAID RESUBMISSION CODE ORIGINAL REF. NO.

23. PRIOR AUTHORIZATION NUMBER

24. A. DATE(S) OF SERVICE From MM DD YY To MM DD YY	B. PLACE OF SERVICE	C. EMG	D. PROCEDURES, SERVICES, OR SUPPLIES (Explain Unusual Circumstances) CPT/HCPCS MODIFIER	E. DIAGNOSIS POINTER	F. $ CHARGES	G. DAYS OR UNITS	H. EPSDT Family Plan	I. ID. QUAL.	J. RENDERING PROVIDER ID. #
1								NPI	
2								NPI	
3								NPI	
4								NPI	
5								NPI	
6								NPI	

25. FEDERAL TAX I.D. NUMBER SSN EIN
26. PATIENT'S ACCOUNT NO.
27. ACCEPT ASSIGNMENT? (For govt. claims, see back) YES NO
28. TOTAL CHARGE $
29. AMOUNT PAID $
30. BALANCE DUE $

31. SIGNATURE OF PHYSICIAN OR SUPPLIER INCLUDING DEGREES OR CREDENTIALS (I certify that the statements on the reverse apply to this bill and are made a part thereof.)

SIGNED DATE

32. SERVICE FACILITY LOCATION INFORMATION a. NPI b.

33. BILLING PROVIDER INFO & PH # ( ) a. NPI b.

PHYSICIAN OR SUPPLIER INFORMATION

NUCC Instruction Manual available at: www.nucc.org

APPROVED OMB-0938-0999 FORM CMS-1500 (08-05)

Figure AIII-1. CMS–1500 form

Block 3: Enter the patient's date of birth in a six-digit format (MM/DD/YY). Enter an "X" in the appropriate box for the patient's gender.

Block 4: Enter the insured's full legal name, beginning with the last name, the first name and middle initial.

- No professional credentials, designations, or periods in this block.
- If the insured is the patient, may enter "Same" in this block.

Block 5: Enter the patient's address and telephone number.

- If using a nine-digit Zip Code to include the rural route, use a hyphen.
- Although a hyphen is not required in manual completion of the form for the telephone number, most software programs are formatted to include a hyphen.
- Do not use commas, periods, or other punctuation marks in this block.

Block 6: Enter an "X" in the correct box indicating the patient's relationship to the insured.

- For worker's compensation claims, check the "Other" box. (Note: For worker's compensation claims, the insured is always the patient's employer.)

Block 7: Enter the insured's address here.

- Do not use commas, periods, or other punctuation in this block.
- If the insured's address is the same as the patient's, may enter "Same."
- For worker's compensation claims, enter the patient's employer's address.

Block 8: Enter the patient's marital and employment status here.

- If the patient is a part-time or full-time student in a postsecondary school or university, check the appropriate box.

Block 9: If Block 11d is checked "YES," complete this block.

- Enter the name of the insured who holds the secondary/supplemental insurance.
- If the insured's name is the same as in Block 2, may leave this block blank.

Block 9a: Enter the policy and/or group number of the secondary/supplemental insurance.

- It is not necessary to include a hyphen or space between the policy and group number for handwritten claims; however, most software programs are formatted to indicate a space between the two numbers.

Block 9b: Enter the date of birth in a six-digit (MM/DD/YY) format for the insured listed in Block 9. Enter an "X" to indicate the gender of the insured listed in Block 9.

Block 9c: Enter the employer's name or school attended by the insured listed in Block 9.

- For Medicare claims, enter "Retired" in this block if the insured listed in Block 9 is retired.

Block 9d: Enter the name of the secondary/supplemental insurance plan or program.

Blocks 10a–10c: Place an "X" in the "NO" box if the patient's condition is not related to employment injury, an automobile accident, or another accident.

- If the patient's condition is the result of an injury that occurred on the job, place an "X" in the "YES" box in 10a.
- If the patient's condition is the result of an automobile accident, place an "X" in the "YES" box in 10b and enter the two-character Postal Service abbreviation in the "(State)" line for the state in which the accident occurred.
- If the patent's condition is the result of another accident (i.e., a fall on the ice outside one's condominium complex), place an "X" in the "YES" box in 10c.

Block 10d: This block is reserved for local use. It is not a data-required field for most claims. Contact individual payers for their guidelines.

- For worker's compensation claims, you may enter the adjuster's name or case manager's name in this block.

Block 11: Enter the primary insurance policy's group number as listed on the health insurance identification card (if one is listed).

- For worker's compensation claims, enter the FECA number (a nine-digit alphanumeric identifier assigned to a patient claiming a work-related condition).
- For Medicare claims, enter the word "None" here.

Block 11a: Enter the insured's (person named in Block 4) date of birth in a six-digit (MM/DD/YY) format. Enter an "X" in the correct box for the insured's gender.

Block 11b: Enter the insured's employer's name or school name here.

- For Medicare claims, enter "Retired" here if the insured is retired.

Block 11c: Enter the primary insurance payer's plan or program name (this may be listed on the health insurance identification card).

- Some payers require an identification number here (contact the individual payer for specific guidelines).
- If no plan or program name is listed on the health insurance identification card and the payer in question does not require data in this block, leave this block blank.

Block 11d: Enter an "X" in the "YES" box if there is health insurance coverage other than the insurance checked in Block 1. (For primary claims, checking "YES" indicates that there is a secondary/supplemental plan.)

- If "YES" is checked, continue and complete boxes 9 through 9d.
- If there is no other health insurance coverage, mark an "X" in the "NO" box.

Block 12: This block is for the patient's or authorized person's signature.

- If a legal signature is not available, enter "Signature on file" or "SOF" in this field, as long as the patient's or authorized person's signature is on file in the medical chart.
- If there is no signature on file, leave blank or enter "No signature on file."
- Enter the date the form was signed or the date of service, in a six-digit (MM/DD/YY) format.

Block 13: Enter the insured's or authorized person's signature here. When signed, the person is requesting that benefits be paid directly to the provider. This is known as "assignment of benefits."

BLOCKS 14–33: PROVIDER OR SUPPLIER INFORMATION

Block 14: This block is used to enter the six-digit (MM/DD/YY) format for the first date of the present illness, injury, or pregnancy.

- For worker's compensation, motor vehicle accidents, or other accidents, enter the date of the injury or accident here.
- For pregnancy claims, enter the date of the patient's last menstrual period (LMP) here.

Block 15: Enter a six-digit (MM/DD/YY) date in this block for the first date the patient had the same or a similar illness.

- Previous pregnancies are not considered a similar illness.
- This block is *not* a required field.
- Leave block blank if original illness date is unknown.

Block 16: If known, enter a six-digit (MM/DD/YY) date in both the "FROM" and "TO" sections of this box, indicating the dates the patient was unable to work in his or her current occupation.

- If the "TO" date is unknown, some software programs will allow "N/A" (not applicable) or no date at all in this field.
- Entry in this block is usually related to a worker's compensation claim.

Block 17: This block is used for the referring provider, the ordering provider, or other source who has referred or ordered the service, or the procedures rendered on the claim.

- Enter the first name, middle initial, last name, and credentials of the referring provider, ordering provider, or other source of services, procedures, or supplies to be billed on the claim.
- Do not enter commas or periods in this block.
- May enter hyphen for hyphenated names.

Block 17a: In the small box to the left, enter the two-character qualifier designated for the identification number (IN) to be entered in the following section. The ID number is a non-NPI provider legacy number.

The provider legacy qualifiers are as follows:

0B	state license number
1B	Blue Shield provider number
1C	Medicare provider number
1D	Medicaid provider number
1G	provider UPIN number
1H	CHAMPUS ID number
E1	employer's ID number
G2	provider commercial number
LU	location number
N5	provider plan network ID number
SY	Social Security number (may not be used for Medicare)
X5	State Industrial Accident provider number
ZZ	provider taxonomy

- As of May 2007, Medicare provider legacy numbers may not be reported on *paper* claims sent to Medicare.

Block 17b: Enter the 10-digit NPI number of the referring provider, ordering provider, performing provider, or other source in this block. As of May 23, 2007, all claims must include the NPI number.

Block 18: Enter the six-digit (MM/DD/YY) hospitalization dates related to current services here.

- This block relates to inpatient stays only. If the patient has not yet been discharged, may enter "N/A" or leave the "TO" field blank.

Block 19: This block may be used when the CPT/HCPCS code billed in Block 24 requires more than four modifiers. Enter the modifiers in this field.

- For Medicare claims, enter the description of the HCPCS level II national code for J codes billed in Block 24 here.
- Contact individual payers for additional claim requirements for this block.

Block 20: Enter an "X" in the "YES" box when billing for purchased services.

- Checking "YES" indicates that the service was performed by an entity other than the billing provider. The other entity will be listed in Block 32.
- Enter the dollar amount under "CHARGES" for the purchased services. Enter "00" to the right of the vertical line if the dollar amount is a whole number.
- Do not enter dollar signs.
- Enter an "X" in the "NO" box when no purchased services are reported on the claim.

Block 21: Enter the patient's diagnosis/condition (ICD-9-CM) code(s) in this block.

- This block may contain up to four ICD-9-CM codes.
- For ICD-9-CM codes containing more than three digits, enter the first three digits before the period and the fourth and fifth (if required) digits after the period.
- For E codes beginning with more than three digits, enter the fourth digit above the period.
- The numbers 1, 2, 3, and 4 listed in this block are referred to as "diagnosis reference numbers" and must correlate to the correct CPT/HCPCS codes billed in Block 24D.

Block 22: This block is used for Medicaid claims.

- Enter the Medicaid resubmission code and original reference number assigned by the Medicaid payer.
- Because Medicaid payers vary by state, contact each payer about its guidelines for this block.

Block 23: Enter any of the following in this block:

- Prior authorization number, if assigned by payer.
- Precertification number, if assigned by payer.
- Clinical Laboratory Improvement Amendments (CLIA) number, if billing for lab services.

Block 24A: Enter the "From" and "To" dates for service(s) rendered.

- Some payers may require a "To" date even when it is the same as the "From" date; it is always advisable to enter both sections to reduce the risk of claim rejection.
- If billing for multiple units for the same service (e.g., follow-up hospital visits for same level of service), may reflect this by listing the "From" date as the first day of the service and the "To" date as the last date this same service was rendered.

Block 24B: Enter the appropriate two-digit place-of-service code for each billable item.

See Table AIII-1.

Table AIII-1. Place-of-Service Codes

Code	Place of Service
03*	School
04*	Homeless shelter
11	Office
12	Home
13**	Assisted living facility
14**	Group home
15*	Mobile unit
20*	Urgent care facility
21	Inpatient hospital
22	Outpatient hospital
23	Emergency room—hospital
24	Ambulatory surgical center (free-standing)
25	Birthing center
26	Military treatment facility
31	Skilled nursing facility (covered Part A stay patient)
32	Nursing facility
33	Custodial care facility
34	Hospice
41	Ambulance (land)
42	Ambulance (air or water)
49**	Independent clinic
50	Federally qualified health center
51	Inpatient psychiatric facility
52	Psychiatric facility partial hospitalization
53	Community mental health center
54	Intermediate care facility/mentally retarded
55	Residential substance abuse treatment facility
56	Psychiatric residential treatment center
57**	Nonresidential substance abuse treatment facility
60	Mass immunization center
61	Comprehensive inpatient rehabilitation facility
62	Comprehensive outpatient rehabilitation facility
65	End-stage renal disease treatment facility
71	State or local public health clinic
72	Rural health clinic
81	Independent laboratory
99	Other unlisted facility

* Valid January 1, 2003, and thereafter.

** Place-of-service code valid October 1, 2003, and thereafter.

Block 24C: This block is used if the service rendered is deemed an "emergency service" (EMG).

- Check the individual payer's requirements for completion of this block. If deemed an emergency, usually a "Y" will be required in this block; if not an emergency, leave blank.

Block 24D: Enter the CPT/HCPCS and modifier (if applicable) code(s) in the unshaded area of this block.

- CPT/HCPCS codes are listed to the left; up to four modifiers may be listed per line item.
- Up to six CPT/HCPCS line items may be billed on one claim form.
- If payers require additional anesthesia services information (e.g., begin and end times) or a narrative description of an unspecified code, enter this information in the shaded area of the block, directly above the CPT/HCPCS code.
- If payers require specific codes (e.g., NCD code for drugs) for durable medical equipment or supplies, enter these codes in the shaded area of the block.

Block 24E: Enter the diagnosis reference number from Block 21 that pertains to each billable line item.

- The primary reference number should always be listed first.
- This block can contain a "1," "2," "3," or "4" or any combination of the four diagnosis reference numbers.
- Do not list the actual ICD-9-CM code in this block.
- Do not use commas to separate the numbers.

Block 24F: Enter the dollar amount for each billable service, procedure, or item.

- Do not enter dollar signs.
- Enter "00" in the cents field to the right of the perforated line if the amount is a whole number.

Block 24G: Enter the number of days or units for the CPT/HCPCS code listed in Block 24D.

- The most common use of this block is for multiple visits, units of supplies, anesthesia units or minutes, or oxygen volume.
- If only one day or unit was needed, enter "1" in this block. If reporting a fraction of a unit, use a decimal point.
- Contact individual payers regarding guidelines for NDC units when using HCPCS billing codes for drugs.

Block 24H: This block is reserved for Medicaid claims.

- If the claim is related to early and periodic screening, diagnosis, treatment, or family planning, enter "Y" for yes.
- Check with each state's Medicaid payers to find out if an "N" is required for non-EPSDT/family planning services.

Block 24I: Enter the non-NPI qualifier as directed in Block 17a (refer to list of qualifiers).

Block 24J: Enter the non-NPI legacy number in the shaded area.

- Enter the 10-digit NPI number in the unshaded area.
- For Medicare claims, report the individual NPI number in the unshaded area when the rendering physician is part of a group practice.
- Use of the NPI number is mandatory as of May 23, 2007.

Block 25: Enter the provider or supplier's tax identification number here (either SSN or EIN) with an "X" in the appropriate box.

- For rendering physicians who are part of a group practice, enter the group's tax identification number.

Block 26: Enter the patient's account number assigned by the provider or supplier's manual or computerized software system.

Block 27: Enter an "X" in the appropriate box.

- An "X" in the "YES" box indicates that the provider has agreed to accept assignment on the claim. An "X" in the "NO" box indicates that the provider does not accept assignment on the claim (a "NO" would indicate that the provider does not have a contract with or does not participate with the payer in question).

Block 28: Enter the total charges from lines 1 through 6 in Block 24F.

- Do not enter dollar signs.
- Enter "00" to the right of the perforated line if the total amount is a whole number.

Block 29: Enter the amount the patient or primary payer paid (for secondary claims).

- Some software programs are not formatted to reflect a patient payment (co-payment or co-insurance) in this block.
- If no payment is made, may leave blank or enter "0" to the left of the perforated line and "00" to the right of the perforated line.

Block 30: Enter the balance-due amount here.

- If the software program used does not reflect an amount in Block 29, this block will equal the dollar amount in Block 28.

Block 31: Enter the signature of the provider or supplier.

- Include degrees or credentials after the name.
- For computerized claims, a printed signature is acceptable.
- "Signature on file" or "SOF" is acceptable in this block.
- Enter the six-digit (MM/DD/YY) date on which the claim was signed or billed (for computerized claims).

Block 32: Enter the name and address of the location where billed items (Block 24D) were rendered.

- If the provider is billing for purchased diagnostic tests, enter the supplier's name and address here.
- If the provider is part of a group practice, enter the name of the group here.
- Do not use commas, periods, or other punctuation in the address.

Block 32a: Enter the NPI of the provider, supplier, or facility listed in Block 32.

Block 32b: Enter the two-digit qualifier (see instructions for Block 17a) followed by the non-NPI legacy number of the provider, supplier, or facility listed in Block 32.

Block 33: Enter the name, address, and telephone number of the billing entity (legal name of the practice) here. If the provider is part of a group practice, enter the group's name here.

Block 33a: Enter the NPI number of the billing entity listed in Block 33. If the billing entity is a group practice, enter the group's NPI number here.

Block 33b: Enter the two-digit qualifier (see instructions for Block 17a) followed by the non-NPI legacy number of the billing entity.

Appendix IV

Patient's Bill of Rights

Patients have the right to:

- Seek consultation with the physician(s) of their choice
- Contract with their physician(s) on mutually agreeable terms
- Be treated confidentially, with access to their records limited to those involved in their care or designated by the patient
- Use their own resources to purchase the care of their choice
- Refuse medical treatment even if it's recommended by their physician
- Be informed about their medical condition, the risks and benefits of treatment and alternatives
- Refuse third-party interference in their medical care, and to be confident that their actions in seeking or declining medical care will not result in third-party imposed penalties for patients or physicians
- Receive full disclosure of their insurance plan in plain language, including:
    - Contracts–A copy of the contract between the physician and the health care plan, and between the patient or employer and the plan
    - Incentives–Whether participating physicians are offered financial incentives to reduce treatment or ration care
    - Cost–The full cost of the plan, including co-payments, co-insurance, and deductibles
    - Coverage–Benefits covered and excluded, including availability and location of 24-hour emergency care

- Qualifications–A roster and qualifications of participating physicians
- Approval procedures–Authorization procedures for services, whether doctor needs approval of a committee or any other individual, and who decides what is medically necessary
- Referrals–Procedures for consulting a specialist and who must authorize the referral
- Appeals–Grievance procedures for claim denials
- Gag rule–Whether physicians are subject to a gag rule, preventing criticism of the plan

Appendix V

Medical Terminology Review by Marie A. Moisio, MA, RHIA

ROOTS, PREFIXES, AND SUFFIXES

Understanding the meaning of roots, prefixes, and suffixes provides a brief definition for many medical terms. A **root** is the foundation of a medical term and usually identifies a body part, color, and sometimes a condition. A **prefix** added to the beginning of a root modifies the meaning of the medical term. A **suffix** added to the end of the root identifies body processes, diseases, abnormal conditions, procedures, and treatments. To define the medical term, start with the meaning of the suffix, the prefix next, and the root last. For example, *hemigastrectomy* means excision of half of the stomach. The suffix *-ectomy* means excision; the prefix *hemi-* means half; and the root *gastr* means stomach. Although a brief definition is helpful, the best place to find the complete definition of all medical terms is in a medical dictionary.

ROOTS

Roots are usually listed with a combining vowel. The combining vowel, usually an *o* and sometimes an *i*, helps ease the pronunciation of medical terms. For example, *gastr/o* indicates that in some medical terms the root *gastr* uses the combining vowel *o*. Some commonly used roots with combining vowels are listed here.

Root	Meaning
abdomin/o	abdomen
aden/o	gland
adren/o; adrenal/o	adrenal gland
aneurysm/o	aneurysm
angi/o	vessel
appendic/o; append/o	appendix
arter/o; arteri/o	artery
arthr/o	joint
ather/o	fat; fatty plaque
bronch/o; bronchi/i	bronchus
burs/o	bursa; sac
cardi/o	heart
cephal/o	head
cerebr/o	cerebrum
cervic/o	cervix
cholangi/o	bile duct
cholecyst/o	gallbladder
choledoch/o	common bile duct
col/o; colon/o	colon
colp/o	vagina
cor/o; coron/o	heart
cost/o	rib
crani/o	cranium; skull
cut/o; cutane/o	skin
cyan/o	blue; bluish
cyst/o	sac; bladder
derm/o; dermat/o	skin
dipl/o	two; double
duoden/o	duodenum
encephal/o	brain
endocrin/o	endocrine
enter/o	intestines
erythr/o	red
esophag/o	esophagus
gastr/o	stomach
gingiv/o	gums
gyn/o; gynec/o	woman
hem/o; hemat/o	blood
hepat/o	liver
hyster/o	uterus
ile/o	ileum
ili/o	ilium; pelvic bone
ir/o; irid/o	iris
jejun/o	jejunum
lapar/o	abdominal wall
laryng/o	larynx
leuk/o	white
lith/o	stone
lymphaden/o	lymph gland
mamm/o; mast/o	breast
my/o	muscle

Root	Meaning
myel/o	bone marrow; spinal cord
myring/o	eardrum
nas/o	nose
nephr/o	kidney
neur/o	nerve
melan/o	black
metr/i; metr/o	uterus
ocul/o	eye
oophor/o	ovary
ophthalm/o	eye
orchi/o; orchid/o	testis; testicle
oste/o	bone
ot/o	ear
ovari/o	ovary
peritone/o	peritoneum
phac/o; phak/o	lens
pharyng/o	pharynx
phleb/o	vein
pleur/o	pleura
pneum/o	air; lung
prostat/o	prostate gland
pulmon/o	lung
pyel/o	renal pelvis
rect/o	rectum
ren/o	kidney
retin/o	retina
rhin/o	nose
salping/o	fallopian tubes; oviducts
scler/o	sclera; hard
sigmoid/o	sigmoid colon
spleen/o	spleen
spondyl/o	vertebral column
stomat/o	mouth
thorac/o	chest; thorax
thromb/o	clot; thrombus
thyr/o; thyroid/o	thyroid gland
trache/o	trachea
tympan/o	eardrum
ur/o	urine; urinary system
ureter/o	ureter
urethra/o	urethra
uter/o	uterus
vagin/o	vagina
vas/o	vessel; vas deferens
ven/o	ven
ventricul/o	ventricle
vertebr/o	vertebra
vesic/o	urinary bladder
xanth/o	yellow

PREFIXES

Prefixes are written with a hyphen following the prefix. Some commonly used prefixes are listed here.

Prefix	Meaning
a-; an-; ana-	no; not; without
ante-	forward
anti-	against
auto-	self
bi-	two; double; both
brady-	slow
dura-	hard
dys-	abnormal; painful
echo-	sound
hemi-	half
hyper-	above; excessive
hypo-	deficient; below
macro-	large
mal-	bad; poor; abnormal
micro-	small
mono-	one
multi-	many
neo-	new
non-	not
nulli-	none
pan-	all
para-	beside; around
per-	through
peri-	around; surrounding
retro-	backward; behind; upward
semi-	half
sub-	below; beneath; under
tachy-	fast
tri-	three
uni-	one

SUFFIXES

Suffixes are written with a hyphen preceding the suffix. Some commonly used suffixes are listed here.

Suffix	Meaning
-algia	pain
-cele	hernia; protrusion
-centesis	surgical puncture
-clasia; clasis	surgical breaking
-cytosis	condition of cells
-desis	binding; fixation
-dynia	pain
-ectasis	stretching; dilation
-ectomy	surgical removal; excision
-emesis	vomiting
-emia	blood condition
-gram	a picture, record; X-ray film
-graph	instrument for recording
-graphy	process of recording
-ia; -iasis	condition; abnormal condition
-itis	inflammation
-lysis; -lytic	destruction; breakdown
-malacia	softening
-megaly	enlarged; enlargement
-metry	measuring; to measure
-oid	like; resembling
-oma	tumor
-opia	vision
-osis	condition
-paresis	partial paralysis
-pathy	disease; illness
-penia	deficiency; decreased number
-pepsia	digestion
-pexy	surgical fixation
-phagia	eating; swallowing
-plasty	surgical repair
-plegia	paralysis
-pnea	breathing
-ptosis	drooping; sagging
-ptysis	spitting up
-(r)rhagia	hemorrhage
-(r)rhaphy	suture of
-(r)rhea	discharge; flow
-(r)rhexis	rupture
-sclerosis	hardening
-scopy	vizualization with a scope
-stenosis	narrowing

Suffix	Meaning
-(o)stomy	creating a new opening
-tomy	incision into
-therapy	treatment
-(o)tocia	labor; birth
-tonia	muscle tone
-tresia	opening
-tripsy	crushing
-uria	urine; urination

Glossary

Accounts receivable: The combined monies due the medical practice from both insurance companies and patients.

Administrative: Duties pertaining to administration.

Age: Growing old; begins once a claim has been submitted.

Allowed amount: The dollar amount an insurance company deems fair for a specific service or procedure.

Appeal letters: Letters submitted to insurance companies requesting reconsideration of payment on a denied claim.

Appeal process: A process used to request reconsideration of a previously denied claim by the insurance company.

Assignment of benefits: Authorization for payment to be made directly to the provider.

Bonding: The act of being protected against financial losses caused by a third party.

Cash flow: A stream of cash (income) used for disbursements.

Centers for Medicare and Medicaid Services (CMS): A governmental agency that oversees the Medicare and Medicaid programs.

Clean claim: A claim with no errors.

Clinical services: The services that involve direct observation and treatment of living patients.

Co-insurance: A percentage amount the patient is responsible to pay for cost of medical services; associated with fee-for-service or traditional plans.

Collecting: The process of claiming what is due and receiving payment. This can actually begin before the patient is ever seen in the medical office.

Collection agencies: Agencies retained for the purpose of collecting debts.

Collections clerk: The person assigned to the ongoing process of collecting accounts receivable.

Contingency fee: The agency is paid its fee only when the account has been successfully paid.

Co-payment: A flat fee the patient pays each time for medical services; associated with managed care plans.

Current Procedural Terminology (CPT): A code that is assigned for services and procedures (code 99080—special reports, such as insurance forms, more than the information conveyed in the usual medical communications or standard reporting form) and that is not reimbursable by most payers.

Customer service: The provision of service to customers (patients) before, during, and after a purchase (service) and is an integral part of both in-home and outsourced (sending work off-site) collections.

Deductible: The dollar amount the patient is responsible to pay before any reimbursement is made by the insurance company.

Delinquent: Past-due.

Denied: Refuse to grant payment for.

Department of Insurance: The governmental agency in charge of controlling and regulating insurance companies.

Deposition: A statement under oath.

Electronic claims: A claim submitted via a computer modem.

Errors and omissions Insurance: Insurance that protects a company from claims if a client holds the company responsible for errors, or the failure of workers to perform as promised in the contract.

Explanation of Benefits (EOB): A form sent by the payer to the physician (or patient) detailing claim benefits.

Fair Debt Collection Practices Act (FDCPA): The primary United States federal law governing debt collection practices. The act stipulates that if a state law is more restrictive than the federal law, the state law will supersede the federal portion of the act.

Federal Reserve Board: The governing body of the central banking system of the United States.

Federal Reserve System: The central banking system of the United States.

Fee schedule: A list of allowed amounts for all services and procedures payable by the insurance company.

Financial policy: A formal set of rules and procedures that the practice follows with regard to collecting money.

Following-up: When medical office personnel calls a payer to check the status of an outstanding claim.

Guarantor: Person financially responsible for the patient's account.

Health insurance claim: A document listing the patient's services, procedures, and diagnoses.

Health Insurance Portability and Accountability Act of 1996 (HIPAA): This law stipulates patients' privacy rights regarding their protected health information.

Health insurance: A contract between the subscriber (the person who "carries" the health insurance) and the insurance company to pay for medical care and preventive services.

Identification number: The number listed on the health insurance card that identifies the patient to the insurance company.

Indemnity plan: A type of insurance plan in which reimbursement is made at 80% of the allowed amount. The patient is then responsible to pay the remaining 20%.

Insurance aging report: A list of claim balances by payers (insurance companies).

Licensing: Formal permission from a governmental or other constituted authority to carry on some business or profession.

Maintaining: Keeping the office's accounts receivable current.

Managed care plan: A health insurance plan that includes financing management and delivery of health care services; usually requires a co-payment.

Medical expert witness: A medical expert who provides services from medical review through trial testimony.

Medicare: A government plan, in which reimbursement for most services and procedures is paid at 80% of the allowed amount.

Narrative report: A report that provides information to insurance carriers, other healthcare professionals, attorneys, and the court system.

New patient: One who has never been seen before or who has not been seen in the past 36 months.

Non-covered benefit: Not a covered benefit in a payer's master benefit list.

CODING BASICS

NPI (National Provider Identifier): A 10-digit number identifying the provider to the payer.

Outsourced: A process of sending work off-site.

Outstanding: Health insurance claims that have not yet been paid or denied.

Paper claims: Claims printed and sent by mail.

Patient aging report: A list showing patient due balances owed to the provider.

Patient registration form: A form used to gather all patient information, including demographics and insurance information.

Patient statement: A bill reflecting the patient's responsibility for payment.

Payers: Insurance companies.

Payment arrangement: A mutually agreed upon dollar amount to be paid (usually monthly) until the balance is paid in full.

Post-dated check: A check dated for the future.

Prompt payment statutes: These are guidelines for timely payment of a health insurance claim.

Re-billing: The process of re-submitting an outstanding claim is called re-billing.

Self-pays: Patients without health insurance and who must pay out-of-pocket for medical care are called self-pays.

State insurance commissioner: The appointed official in charge of each state's Department of Insurance.

Subscriber: The person who "carries" the health insurance.

Superbill: A form listing CPT, HCPCS, and ICD-9 codes used to record services performed for the patient and the patient's diagnosis(es) for a given visit.

Supplemental plan: A secondary insurance plan intended to cover the cost of the patient's deductible and/or 20% co-insurance.

Surety bonds: Promise of performance.

Traditional plan: If the patient has an indemnity plan, also known as a traditional plan, the insurance company is usually responsible to pay 80% of the allowed amount.

Unauthorized: Authorization or approval not obtained prior to treatment.

Uninsured: Patients without health insurance coverage.

Index

A

Accounts receivable, 9, 27, 29
Administrative duties, 74
Aging process, 9, 24
Aging reports
  insurance, 27, 28
  patient, 34–36
Allowed amount, 46
Appeal process, 11, 61–68
Appeals documentation, 65–68
Assignment of benefits, 7

B

Bonding, 90

C

Cash flow, 36
Centers for Medicare and Medicaid Services (CMS), 84
Checks, post-dated, 45, 49
Claim submittal, 9
Claims
  aging process, 9, 24
  appealing denied, 62–68
  clean, 24
  denied, 62
  electronic, 23
  following-up on, 29–31
  outstanding, 27
  paper, 24
  reasons for unpaid, 29
Clean claims, 24
Clinical services, 73
CMS-1500 form, 9, 10
Co-insurance, 4, 46
Collecting
  defined, 4
  legal guidelines for, 15–18
Collection agencies, 16
  communication with, 94
  fees charged by, 94
  role of, 90
  selecting, 90
  techniques used by, 90–94
Collection calls, 52
Collection practices
  FAQs about, 16–17
  prohibited, 17–18
Collection process
  claim submittal, 9
  financial policy and, 5–8
  overview of, 4–5
Collection strategies, in-office patient, 45–56
Collection techniques, 90–93
Collections clerk, role of, 9
Communications
  with collection agency, 94
  effective, 11
  nonverbal, 11
Complaint forms, 32–34
Complaints, 32–34
Consistency, in follow-up, 36
Contingency-fee basis, 94
Co-payments, 4, 46–47
Copies of medical records, 74
Credit cards, 49
Current Procedural Terminology (CPT) code, 74
Customer service
  collection agency, 94
  plan for, 11
  role of, in collections, 9, 11

D

Debit cards, 46
Debt collectors. *See also* Collection agencies
  prohibited practices, 17–18
Deductible, 4
Delinquent accounts, 90
Denied claims, 62
  appeals process for, 62–68
  reasons for, 62, 64
  suggested actions for, 64
Department of Insurance, 31
Department of Insurance complaint form, 32–34

E

Electronic claims, 24
Errors and omissions insurance, 90
Expert witness, 84–85
Explanation of Benefits (EOB), 62–63

F

Fair Debt Collections Practices Act (FDCPA), 16–18, 90
Federal regulations, 16
Federal Reserve Board, 16
Federal Reserve System, 16
Fee schedules, 46
Fees
- collection agency, 94
- medical expert witness, 84–85
- for missed appointments, 75, 84

Financial policy, 5–8
Follow-up, 29
Follow-up techniques, 30–31, 36–37
Form completion, 74

G

Guarantor, 5

H

Health insurance card, 48
Health insurance claim form, 10
Health insurance claims. *See* Claims
Health insurance identification card, 4, 5
Health Insurance Portability and Accountability Act (HIPAA), 17
Health insurance, verification, 4, 46–48

I

Identification number, health insurance, 4
Income sources, supplemental, 74–85
Indemnity plans, 46
In-office patient collection strategies, 45–56
- forms of payment, 48–50
- health insurance verification, 46–48
- patient statements, 49–52
- telephone calls to patients, 52

Insurance aging reports, 27, 28
Insurance companies
- complaints against, 31–34
- regulation of, 31–34

Interest, 17
Internet, checking claims on, 29

L

Legal guidelines, for collecting, 15–18
Licensing, 90

M

Managed care plans, 46
Medical debt, 16
Medical expert witness, 84–85
Medical information, disclosure of, 17
Medical office personnel, suggested courses of action for, 30
Medical records copying, 74
Medicare, 46, 62–63
Missed appointment fees, 75, 84

N

Narrative reports, 74, 75, 77–84
National Provider Identifier (NPI), 30
New patients, 4–5
No-fault claims, 16
Non-covered benefits, 62, 64
Nonverbal communication, 11

O

Outsourced collections, 9
Outstanding claims
- defined, 27
- re-billing, 31

Overdue bills, interest on, 17

P

Paper claims, 24
Past-due accounts, 90
Patient aging reports, 34–36
Patient registration, 4–5
Patient registration form, 5, 6
Patient statements, 46, 49–51
Patients
- calling, 51
- communication with, 11
- contacting, 16–17
- new, 4–5
- privacy rights of, 17
- uninsured, 35, 48

Payers, 27
Payment arrangement contract, 50
Payment arrangements, 49
Payment forms, 49
Post-dated checks, 49
Privacy rights, 17
Prohibited practices, 17–18
Prompt payment statutes, 24–28

R

Re-billing, 31
Regulations
- on debt collecting, 16
- on insurance companies, 31–34

"Release of Information," 75, 76
Role-playing activities, 36–37, 53–55

S

Self-pays, 4
State insurance commissioner, 31
State regulations, 16
Subscriber, 4
Superbill, 46
Supplemental income sources, 74–85

Supplemental plans, 46
Surety bonds, 90

T

Telephone calls, for following-up claims, 30
Traditional plans, 46

U

Unauthorized services, 62, 64
Uninsured patients, 35, 49
Unpaid claims
  reasons for, 30
  suggested courses of action for, 30

W

Worker's compensation claims, 16

IMPORTANT! READ CAREFULLY: This End User License Agreement ("Agreement") sets forth the conditions by which Cengage Learning will make electronic access to the Cengage Learning-owned licensed content and associated media, software, documentation, printed materials, and electronic documentation contained in this package and/or made available to you via this product (the "Licensed Content"), available to you (the "End User"). BY CLICKING THE "I ACCEPT" BUTTON AND/OR OPENING THIS PACKAGE, YOU ACKNOWLEDGE THAT YOU HAVE READ ALL OF THE TERMS AND CONDITIONS, AND THAT YOU AGREE TO BE BOUND BY ITS TERMS, CONDITIONS, AND ALL APPLICABLE LAWS AND REGULATIONS GOVERNING THE USE OF THE LICENSED CONTENT.

1.0 SCOPE OF LICENSE

1.1 Licensed Content. The Licensed Content may contain portions of modifiable content ("Modifiable Content") and content which may not be modified or otherwise altered by the End User ("Non-Modifiable Content"). For purposes of this Agreement, Modifiable Content and Non-Modifiable Content may be collectively referred to herein as the "Licensed Content." All Licensed Content shall be considered Non-Modifiable Content, unless such Licensed Content is presented to the End User in a modifiable format and it is clearly indicated that modification of the Licensed Content is permitted.

1.2 Subject to the End User's compliance with the terms and conditions of this Agreement, Cengage Learning hereby grants the End User, a nontransferable, nonexclusive, limited right to access and view a single copy of the Licensed Content on a single personal computer system for noncommercial, internal, personal use only. The End User shall not (i) reproduce, copy, modify (except in the case of Modifiable Content), distribute, display, transfer, sublicense, prepare derivative work(s) based on, sell, exchange, barter or transfer, rent, lease, loan, resell, or in any other manner exploit the Licensed Content; (ii) remove, obscure, or alter any notice of Cengage Learning's intellectual property rights present on or in the Licensed Content, including, but not limited to, copyright, trademark, and/or patent notices; or (iii) disassemble, decompile, translate, reverse engineer, or otherwise reduce the Licensed Content.

2.0 TERMINATION

2.1 Cengage Learning may at any time (without prejudice to its other rights or remedies) immediately terminate this Agreement and/or suspend access to some or all of the Licensed Content, in the event that the End User does not comply with any of the terms and conditions of this Agreement. In the event of such termination by Cengage Learning, the End User shall immediately return any and all copies of the Licensed Content to Cengage Learning.

3.0 PROPRIETARY RIGHTS

3.1 The End User acknowledges that Cengage Learning owns all rights, title and interest, including, but not limited to all copyright rights therein, in and to the Licensed Content, and that the End User shall not take any action inconsistent with such ownership. The Licensed Content is protected by U.S., Canadian and other applicable copyright laws and by international treaties, including the Berne Convention and the Universal Copyright Convention. Nothing contained in this Agreement shall be construed as granting the End User any ownership rights in or to the Licensed Content.

3.2 Cengage Learning reserves the right at any time to withdraw from the Licensed Content any item or part of an item for which it no longer retains the right to publish, or which it has reasonable grounds to believe infringes copyright or is defamatory, unlawful, or otherwise objectionable.

4.0 PROTECTION AND SECURITY

4.1 The End User shall use its best efforts and take all reasonable steps to safeguard its copy of the Licensed Content to ensure that no unauthorized reproduction, publication, disclosure, modification, or distribution of the Licensed Content, in whole or in part, is made. To the extent that the End User becomes aware of any such unauthorized use of the Licensed Content, the End User shall immediately notify Cengage Learning. Notification of such violations may be made by sending an e-mail to infringement@cengage.com.

5.0 MISUSE OF THE LICENSED PRODUCT

5.1 In the event that the End User uses the Licensed Content in violation of this Agreement, Cengage Learning shall have the option of electing liquidated damages, which shall include all profits generated by the End User's use of the Licensed Content plus interest computed at the maximum rate permitted by law and all legal fees and other expenses incurred by Cengage Learning in enforcing its rights, plus penalties.

6.0 FEDERAL GOVERNMENT CLIENTS

6.1 Except as expressly authorized by Cengage Learning, Federal Government clients obtain only the rights specified in this Agreement and no other rights. The Government acknowledges that (i) all software and related documentation incorporated in the Licensed Content is existing commercial computer software within the meaning of FAR 27.405(b)(2); and (2) all other data delivered in whatever form, is limited rights data within the meaning of FAR 27.401. The restrictions in this section are acceptable as consistent with the Government's need for software and other data under this Agreement.

7.0 DISCLAIMER OF WARRANTIES AND LIABILITIES

7.1 Although Cengage Learning believes the Licensed Content to be reliable, Cengage Learning does not guarantee or warrant (i) any information or materials contained in or produced by the Licensed Content, (ii) the accuracy, completeness or reliability of the Licensed Content, or (iii) that the Licensed Content is free from errors or other material defects. THE LICENSED PRODUCT IS PROVIDED "AS IS," WITHOUT ANY WARRANTY OF ANY KIND AND CENGAGE LEARNING DISCLAIMS ANY AND ALL WARRANTIES, EXPRESSED OR IMPLIED, INCLUDING, WITHOUT LIMITATION, WARRANTIES OF MERCHANTABILITY OR FITNESS FOR A PARTICULAR PURPOSE. IN NO EVENT SHALL CENGAGE LEARNING BE LIABLE FOR: INDIRECT, SPECIAL, PUNITIVE OR CONSEQUENTIAL DAMAGES INCLUDING FOR LOST PROFITS, LOST DATA, OR OTHERWISE. IN NO EVENT SHALL CENGAGE LEARNING'S AGGREGATE LIABILITY HEREUNDER, WHETHER ARISING IN CONTRACT, TORT, STRICT LIABILITY OR OTHERWISE, EXCEED THE AMOUNT OF FEES PAID BY THE END USER HEREUNDER FOR THE LICENSE OF THE LICENSED CONTENT.

8.0 GENERAL

8.1 Entire Agreement. This Agreement shall constitute the entire Agreement between the Parties and supercedes all prior Agreements and understandings oral or written relating to the subject matter hereof.

8.2 Enhancements/Modifications of Licensed Content. From time to time, and in Cengage Learning's sole discretion, Cengage Learning may advise the End User of updates, upgrades, enhancements and/or improvements to the Licensed Content, and may permit the End User to access and use, subject to the terms and conditions of this Agreement, such modifications, upon payment of prices as may be established by Cengage Learning.

8.3 No Export. The End User shall use the Licensed Content solely in the United States and shall not transfer or export, directly or indirectly, the Licensed Content outside the United States.

8.4 Severability. If any provision of this Agreement is invalid, illegal, or unenforceable under any applicable statute or rule of law, the provision shall be deemed omitted to the extent that it is invalid, illegal, or unenforceable. In such a case, the remainder of the Agreement shall be construed in a manner as to give greatest effect to the original intention of the parties hereto.

8.5 Waiver. The waiver of any right or failure of either party to exercise in any respect any right provided in this Agreement in any instance shall not be deemed to be a waiver of such right in the future or a waiver of any other right under this Agreement.

8.6 Choice of Law/Venue. This Agreement shall be interpreted, construed, and governed by and in accordance with the laws of the State of New York, applicable to contracts executed and to be wholly preformed therein, without regard to its principles governing conflicts of law. Each party agrees that any proceeding arising out of or relating to this Agreement or the breach or threatened breach of this Agreement may be commenced and prosecuted in a court in the State and County of New York. Each party consents and submits to the nonexclusive personal jurisdiction of any court in the State and County of New York in respect of any such proceeding.

8.7 Acknowledgment. By opening this package and/or by accessing the Licensed Content on this Web site, THE END USER ACKNOWLEDGES THAT IT HAS READ THIS AGREEMENT, UNDERSTANDS IT, AND AGREES TO BE BOUND BY ITS TERMS AND CONDITIONS. IF YOU DO NOT ACCEPT THESE TERMS AND CONDITIONS, YOU MUST NOT ACCESS THE LICENSED CONTENT AND RETURN THE LICENSED PRODUCT TO CENGAGE LEARNING (WITHIN 30 CALENDAR DAYS OF THE END USER'S PURCHASE) WITH PROOF OF PAYMENT ACCEPTABLE TO CENGAGE LEARNING, FOR A CREDIT OR A REFUND. Should the End User have any questions/comments regarding this Agreement, please contact Cengage Learning at Delmar.help@cengage.com.